Contents

Introduction 5

Chapter 1: The Teacher/Student Disconnect 10
The Demands of School 10
The Boring Stuff 19

Chapter 2: Connecting Your Worldview to Theirs 22
An Invisible Disability 23
Challenges in Perspective-Taking 25
   Literal Thinking 27
Strategies to Build Perspective-Taking 30
   Short, Engaging Activities 31
   Language, Social Studies, and the Arts 31
   Science, Health, and Math 32
   Physical Education 33
   Social Situations 34

Chapter 3: Connecting the Dots 36
The Hidden Curriculum 38
Generalizing Skills and Situations 40
Cognitive Learning Style 43
Strategies to Help Connect the Dots 45

Chapter 4: The Power of Personal Connection 47
Fostering Positive Rapport 49
Social Differences 52
   Bullying 53
   Long-Term Outcomes 56
   The Social Gap 56
Strategies for Unstructured Times 57
   Group Work 57
   Recess 58
   Maintaining an Inclusive Climate 59

Chapter 5: Connecting the Pieces 62
Information Processing 63
   Weak Central Coherence 63
   Executive Dysfunction 63
Language Processing 65
Teaching Strategies 67
   Say What You Mean and Mean What You Say 67

Help to Pinpoint What's Important   *68*
Planning and Organization   *72*
Structure for Success   *74*

Chapter 6: Connecting Sensory, Anxiety, and Emotional Regulation   *80*

Sensory Processing   *80*
Dealing with Big Feelings   *82*
Structuring the Classroom Environment   *86*
Physical Layout   *86*
Sensory Accommodations   *86*
Classroom Culture   *87*
Strategies for Emotional Regulation   *88*
Talk Accurately about Emotions   *88*
Teach New Strategies   *89*
Model Self-Care   *90*

Chapter 7: Connecting the *Why* to Behaviors   *91*

Thinking Productively about Behaviors   *91*
Words to Say   *92*
When to Stop Talking   *92*
Crisis Management   *93*
Discovering the *Why?*   *94*
Deciding the *Now What?*   *95*
What Doesn't Work   *95*
Types of Consequences that Work   *95*
Strategies for Maximizing Outcomes   *98*
Ongoing Check-ins and Goal-Setting   *98*
Giving Attention   *100*
Using Accountability Language   *102*

Chapter 8: Connecting through Strengths and Interests   *108*

Grabbing and Holding Student Interest   *109*
Effective Reward Systems   *110*
Possible Rewards   *111*
Your Expectations   *111*
The Earning Schedule   *111*
Using a Reward System to Support Child Success   *112*
Strategies for Building Student Self-Esteem and Relationships   *114*
Interests Can Help Increase Awareness of Others   *114*
Treat Them Like Experts   *115*

Final Thoughts   *119*

Acknowledgments   *120*

Professional Resources   *123*

Recommended Resources   *123*
References   *126*

Index   *133*

The Autism Lens

Everything teachers need
to connect with students, build confidence,
and promote classroom learning

KARA DYMOND

Pembroke Publishers Limited

For Danny
and for all the students he inspired me to teach

Stock images in the book are free for commercial use, no attribution required, and sourced from Pixabay, Unsplash, and Adobe Stock.

© 2020 Pembroke Publishers
538 Hood Road
Markham, Ontario, Canada L3R 3K9
www.pembrokepublishers.com

All rights reserved.
No part of this publication may be reproduced in any form or by any means electronic or mechanical, including photocopy, scanning, recording, or any information, storage or retrieval system, without permission in writing from the publisher. Excerpts from this publication may be reproduced under licence from Access Copyright, or with the express written permission of Pembroke Publishers Limited, or as permitted by law.

Every effort has been made to contact copyright holders for permission to reproduce borrowed material. The publishers apologize for any such omissions and will be pleased to rectify them in subsequent reprints of the book.

Library and Archives Canada Cataloguing in Publication

Title: The autism lens : everything teachers need to connect with students, build confidence, and promote classroom learning / Kara Dymond.

Names: Dymond, Kara, author.

Description: Includes bibliographical references and index.

Identifiers: Canadiana (print) 20200290851 | Canadiana (ebook) 20200291378 | ISBN 9781551383477 (softcover) | ISBN 9781551389479 (PDF)

Subjects: LCSH: Autistic children—Education.

Classification: LCC LC4717 .D96 2020 | DDC 371.94dc23

Editor: Kat Mototsune
Cover Design: John Zehethofer
Typesetting: Jay Tee Graphics Ltd.

Printed and bound in Canada
9 8 7 6 5 4 3 2 1

Introduction

Let me tell you how I first became aware of the autism lens, long before I ever heard of autism. When I was in middle school, my younger brother Danny struggled in the mainstream classroom. He had difficulty understanding what was being asked of him, making eye contact, and speaking in full sentences unless it was about dinosaurs or video games, and he spent all his recesses hugging me. It took years for Danny to get an autism diagnosis and, like many children on waiting lists for assessments, he was an enigma to school staff. Well-intentioned teachers spoke louder in their attempts to elicit an answer, which sent his brain into a panic. Some would surround him with helpful peers, whose endless chatter, directions, and movements blurred together into sensory overload for him. Others interpreted his minimal eye contact and inability to say "I don't understand" or "I need help" as willful defiance.

One day, while passing by his Grade 2 classroom, I heard the raised voice of Danny's teacher. "Well? Answer me!"

I clung to the attendance sheet as I peeked inside, searching the room to see who was in trouble. Everyone was looking at Danny. His face was frozen, his cheeks red, his eyes boring into the floor. His entire body looked withered. The teacher repeated her demand for a response. *Doesn't she understand?* I thought. *He can't!*

There is nothing worse for students or teachers than feeling powerless. Today, as a teacher myself, I have sympathy for Danny's teachers and support staff, who were baffled and trying anything—everything—they could, at a time when there weren't many resources to help them understand what was going on in Danny's brain. I didn't have the words for it then, but Danny helped me glimpse the fact that what we often assume to be misbehavior is really an indication of something the student doesn't understand or can't do *yet*.

That was the moment it became my mission to help Danny meet success while learning. I wanted his entire class to see what he could do, not just what he couldn't. He'd sit through almost any math problem if Mario and Luigi (his favorite Nintendo characters) made an appearance. I taught him to swim underwater by pretending we were in a video game, diving for coins. Little did I know, at the time, how much I was learning about good teaching!

Though it wasn't a surprise to anyone but me, I became a teacher. For almost ten years, I have taught students with autism in a specialized withdrawal program, three days a week. The rest of the week, I'm an autism consultant—planning, visiting schools, collaborating with teachers and families, designing and delivering professional development, and developing tools and strategies to help my students across settings. I have grown exponentially as a teacher because of the rich interactions with colleagues. And some of my biggest breakthroughs have come from my students. All of my personal and professional experiences have contributed to my autism lens.

It hasn't been easy. I've encountered many difficult-to-connect-with students. In the challenging moments, it has been downright miserable. In my first year, I was shocked to realize there were kids I didn't look forward to working with. I worked hard not to show it and, each day on my drive to school, I recited the mantra: "The children who need love the most will always ask for it in the most unloving ways" (Barkley, 2000, p. 5). Over time, I shifted my attention to relationship-building and saw the positives increase and the negatives decrease. Once we got to the other side of the tough moments, and once I learned how to avoid most power struggles, I discovered how much I love teaching these kids! Figuring out what makes them tick and teaching them more adaptive skills has not only brought me tremendous joy, it's also improved my teaching.

The Teacher–Student Connection

The power of the teacher–student connection is at the heart of this book. As teachers, we *know* it's important to connect with students. We *know* having a good relationship makes everything else easier. We've read all the books and heard it in our teacher preparation courses. As real, on-the-ground teachers, we also know this isn't as easy as it sounds. How and where do we start?

Every so often in teaching, we experience a transformative shift in awareness, a short distance but a giant leap from head to heart. I'll never forget my student Alberto. He had recently learned he had autism and was struggling to accept his diagnosis. His struggle was aggravated by the fact that I had recently replaced the teacher he'd had for two years. Eyeing me up and down, Alberto turned to Sonia Tran, our incredible class Child and Youth Worker, to loudly ask, "Do YOU like her?" When other kids gave me hugs, he scoffed.

Over several months, Alberto sized me up, gauging my reaction to different scenarios. During lessons, his contributions were variations of "So what?" or "That's stupid." As a beginning teacher, I barely had a handle on the curriculum, never mind trying to puzzle out how to calm a twelve-year-old, already the size of a football player, who seemed intent on not fitting into the group on any level. Alberto was the only student who ever gave me a swift kick to the shin. It was a tentative and testing kind of kick, but a surprise nonetheless. I wasn't as good at de-escalating or teaching proactively as I am now. It seemed Sonia and I were endlessly problem-solving as a team how to get the buy-in or to teach the self-regulation skills he needed.

One day over the lunch hour, I heard him join a conversation that piqued my interest. He wanted to try rock climbing. On my planning time, I Googled "rock climbing for kids" and found a place a short bus ride away. The next week, I announced our upcoming field trip to the class. I still get chills when I think about it: the moment when theory settled deeply within my heart. The moment my relationship with Alberto—and his relationship to the entire class—began to change.

Quietly, Alberto looked up at me and said, "No one's ever listened to me before."

I lay awake that night thinking about the importance of listening to students and including their voice in our classrooms. How often do our students with autism get a say in what they do or how they do it? Whether at home, school, or behavioral skills programs, they are micromanaged in so many ways. Yes, of course, teachers *know* they should listen to students. Alberto taught me *why* we should.

How We View Autistic Students

If I asked you to finish the sentence *All autistic children are...*, what would you say? Think, for a moment, about the associations your brain makes when you think of learners with autism. Neurotypical brains—brains that develop the way the majority do—are used to making generalizations to help us predict and interpret future encounters, but that can also be a pitfall, robbing us of the chance to see children as they are.

When I ask you to consider things through an autism lens, I do not mean to imply that all autistic people have the same needs or perspective. There is incredible diversity across the spectrum—no two students I've worked with have had the same combination of strengths and developing areas. Some of the children described in this book are under-the-radar kids who stand out only if you watch closely, particularly at recess. After years of unsuccessfully trying to join in, they sometimes adapt by avoiding interactions entirely and escaping into a book. They worry most of the time about how others perceive them and struggle to participate in groups; they have difficulty communicating in a way that is received well by others or even understanding why others conform to the many unexplained rules of school and other settings. Other students with autism featured in this book need more obvious supports, requiring considerable prompting to complete work; they are much less able to interpret people's reactions in any situation. They might invade the personal space of classmates or teachers, rigidly point out rule violations, or get up to investigate the reading area during a lesson, unaware of their impact on those around them. At recess, they may try repeatedly to join groups of kids who show nonverbal cues of lack of interest or they may submerge so fully into their imaginations that they obliviously jump and leap through the middle of their peers' basketball game. All my students struggle with recognizing their own powder keg of emotions and how to express these emotions in productive ways. Some have meltdowns in front of the class, while some bottle up what they are feeling and explode at home after a day of keeping themselves together. All day, they are working harder than most people recognize.

When I use the term *autism lens*, I am not suggesting there is only one way to respond to learners on the autism spectrum. If that were true, evidence-based practices would always work or always be enough. Every parent or educator knows that the same thing does not work for everybody because all children, with autism or without, are complex. While this book will share some generalizations from autism research, the learners in your class won't all fit in neatly to the studies you've read, just as research into women or middle children doesn't accurately encompass all that is me.

Introduction   7

Nor am I implying that we view learners with autism as vastly different from other learners in our classrooms. Have you noticed how, when we are talking about a child with an exceptionality, we often focus on their weaknesses? Every person has things they're good at and things they're not so good at. Children with autism can sometimes perform as well as—or outperform—so-called "neuro-typical" students. They can share characteristics that overlap with students with other recognized needs, such as being gifted, having ADHD, having sensory-processing disorder, and having nonverbal learning disabilities.

Rather than imposing restrictions on how we view our learners with autism, the title of this book, *The Autism Lens*, is an invitation to see each learner holistically while recognizing that many challenges exist for autistic students in school settings and learning what kinds of strategies can be adapted to mitigate these challenges. Once I gleaned a brain-based understanding of why our expectations and classroom environments might need to shift so our students with autism can meet their potential, it was easier to shed unhelpful associations that limited my perspective.

An informed autism lens will help you to envision each student with autism as they are and as they can be. Soften your focus a little on those developing areas. Instead, focus more sharply on what they are able to do and what they can bring to the table. Strengths can bolster what students need to learn. With practice, it gets easier to filter your classroom through an autism lens. It's almost impossible to do when students—and teachers—are in the middle of a really tough time. But even an impasse can be an invitation and an opportunity. Try to see it their way. Trade lenses, for a moment. That way, you may learn what you need to teach—and reach—them.

Why I Wrote This Book

As an autism consultant, I have listened and learned from hundreds of educators. We've talked about the anxiety we all experience when left alone to figure out how to support students with autism. As I have delivered and researched effective teacher professional development, time and again educators have said they are tired of teaching through trial and error. They don't want more research or government documents, although these can certainly be worthwhile.

This book is the outcome of years of conversations with teachers, support staff, teacher candidates, and parents, and of what they've repeatedly told me they want to understand better. Educators want to move beyond diagnostic criteria to recognize what autism really means for students' learning and development. They want to hear what works for other teachers and find teacher-tested strategies and resources they can easily apply in their own classrooms.

Through my many collaborations with school staff, we've swapped stories about our students and the moments when our own perspectives have been expanded. We have worked together to develop creative, individualized interventions for specific students, as well as whole-class approaches to differentiate instruction and build relationships. I've stepped into classrooms and been wowed by teachers paying careful attention to group dynamics to see who is being left out and finding creative ways to build that child up. I've admired teachers whose organizational skills far surpass my own, who have established innovative systems to help our "tornado" students keep their desks clean and file loose sheets away. I've collected hundreds of tips, tricks, and best practices from my colleagues. This book aims to share these insights with you, teacher to teacher, to remove some of the guesswork. It doesn't require a complete overhaul of what you're already doing well. The most exciting part is that many of these suggestions will benefit the learning, attention, social abilities, and self-regulation of your entire class!

Why Read This Book?

We have tremendous impact on our students' quality of life. Their well-being and peace of mind is profoundly connected to our own. I hope this book contributes to your peace of mind, providing you with practical solutions to reduce any anxiety about how to meet the needs of students with autism, and moves you from apprehension to an appreciation of the strengths of these students. The magic of being a teacher is that we grow and transform through our interactions with our students. I hope you experience this. More than anything, I hope this book will help you give yourself permission to nurture, support, and engage students in creative ways that work for you and your classroom. You'll catch glimpses of my students, whose voices and stories are interwoven through this book. Together, we will unpack the kinds of challenges that might manifest in your classroom and why. We'll review how to anticipate these challenges and develop strategies for nipping them in the bud.

Take a deep breath and stop worrying. It's okay not to know what to do. You just need to know where to begin. And we begin by connecting. This book will help you to see that connection starts when we bend to see from our students' points of view and gain their trust. Once we learn how our students with autism might think and perceive the world, we can better understand the changes to make to have powerful impact. Then we can nudge these students into the space where learning can happen. You've got this! In case no one's ever told you, you can confidently meet all children where they are and support them along their own unique trajectory. Just take it one connection at a time.

1

The Teacher/Student Disconnect

Works fundamental to my practice and my philosophy include the books and the Collaborative and Proactive Solutions approach to behavior developed by Dr. Ross Greene (livesinthebalance.org); *The Complete Guide to Asperger's Syndrome* by Dr. Tony Attwood (2007); the notion of the "hidden curriculum" as described by Dr. Brenda Smith Myles and colleagues (2004); and the Social Thinking® Methodology created by Michelle Garcia Winner (www.socialthinking. com). Starting on page 123 you will find recommended resources for exploring related topics, and suggestions for classroom read-alouds to reinforce perspective-taking, inclusion, social-emotional awareness, and autism understanding with students.

Teaching is tough. I'm sure if you work in a school, you'll agree: until I became a teacher, I had no idea how much educators invest in our classrooms and students. Growing up, it didn't register how hard it must be to teach a diverse group of learners and to help each student along their own pathway to success. My autistic brother Danny switched to an independent school by Grade 3 and no one else in my school appeared to have any disabilities or learning differences. I didn't see them, but that doesn't mean they weren't there.

The landscape of schools has changed in the years since then. There are so many more needs in our classrooms to understand, accommodate, and support that it can be overwhelming. It's not just supporting students with identified exceptionalities that concerns teachers. The invisible load many students carry into the classroom has a very tangible impact on their mental health, well-being, and ability to learn. I work with colleagues whose hearts are bigger than their wallets, who stock their classrooms with snacks for the students going without, and who pitch in to buy a new snowsuit and winter boots for the kid who has none. Our profession is filled with educators who notice and care, and we take it all home with us. Faces scroll through our brains at night as, instead of counting sheep, we fret about whether we're doing enough to foster inclusion, to differentiate to support the range of learners, to get to the root of challenging behaviors, to motivate a heel-dragger, to slow down a roadrunner, or to facilitate independence. We constantly ask ourselves, *Is there anyone who is falling through the cracks?*

The Demands of School

When students with autism are young, school is usually highly structured. They benefit from explicit instruction combining verbal, step-by-step instruction with visual exemplars; scaffolding of tasks; student repetition of those instructions;

10   *The Teacher/Student Disconnect*

and lots and lots of practice of skills. Compared to when they are in later grades, children in primary classrooms more frequently produce individual work and encounter a greater emphasis on rote learning of the basics, even in highly hands-on and centres-based classrooms. This allows autistic students to use their strong logical and rule-bound thinking and to feel successful. They often have show and tell, where they can dazzle teachers and peers with their enormous knowledge of their favorite topics. When educators use strengths and a positive relationship to motivate and encourage, students love coming to school.

As these students move up into middle school, they are at greater risk of falling through the cracks. They are expected to have a level of mastery over some thinking skills that are thought to be core difficulties of autism: perspective-taking (see Chapter 2), generalizing and context blindness (see Chapter 3), executive function and seeing what's important (see Chapter 5), and sensory and emotional regulation (see Chapter 6). The curriculum tends to require them to infer, predict, decipher causal relationships, connect, interpret meaning, think critically, and see from others' points of view (Garcia Winner, 2013). I once opened the Grade 6 language curriculum and highlighted any expectation that would be contingent on these particular skills. The pages were soon a sea of neon pink! To complicate matters, assessment activities become even more social with each passing grade. Students participate in presentations, group projects, inquiry-based learning, and classroom discussions. Teachers take a step back, expecting their students to take greater ownership over their learning. Instruction becomes less explicit and is often delivered verbally in multiple steps, and students are assumed to possess certain prerequisite skills that have been absorbed intuitively over their years in school. They are faced with open-ended questions, choices, and tasks that can be approached more than one way and still must somehow be correct. They must transition not just between subjects, but between rooms and teachers, bringing the right materials with them to each class. And the classroom rules—those hidden rules—are always changing! If we fail to connect or notice what's going on for students with autism, it can have long-term implications.

Let's put on our autism lens for a moment. To get a better sense of what school can feel like for students with autism, we'll examine two hypothetical children who are composites of many students I've supported. Gino is in Grade 3, carries a Pokémon plush doll with him everywhere, and always knows the weather report. Annie is in Grade 7, loves K-pop and anime, and is teaching herself to speak Korean (she is not Korean). As you read, think about what strengths and developing areas you can identify.

Pseudonyms are used for all students mentioned throughout this book.

	Gino's Day	**Annie's Day**
8:30 a.m.	Gino is still in his mother's car. It's a cloudy day, and he is afraid of rain. His family once went camping and they were caught in a thunderstorm; he screamed all night. Now, no amount of bribery or force can get him to brave a storm, and cloudy days are almost as bad. As usual, a struggle ensues to get him out the door and into the car, and then out of the car and into the school. He is late entering the building, his whole body taut with tension.	The school bell rings. Annie has been waiting for the bell. She doesn't feel comfortable joining the groups of her peers in the yard before school, so she waits against the wall where her class lines up, listening to K-pop with her headphones on. She is always first in line. As her peers bump and cluster into line, she doesn't look around. She doesn't say hi to anyone; what if they don't say hi back?

The Demands of School 11

8:45 a.m.	Gino storms into the classroom, even though the teacher is teaching about procedural writing. "I hate school!" he yells. The teacher tells him to come in again, more politely. He refuses, more loudly. There is a collective inhale as the other students anticipate a showdown, but the teacher takes a breath and asks the educational assistant, Miss G, to help Gino calm down and unpack his bag. The teacher continues teaching, thankful that Gino has support in a class with many identified needs, four English-language learners, and a handful of students with their own unidentified learning challenges. Miss G prompts every action required of Gino: "Hang up your bag. Unzip it. Take out your books. Zip it back up. Bring your books…" When they are seated at the back of the classroom, Miss G lets Gino talk about Pokémon for a few minutes. He becomes animated and the morning stress washes away. Finally, Miss G says, "It's time to open up your spelling notebook. We're going to continue what we were doing yesterday." Gino complies right away.	Annie unzips her bag and everything falls out. Some of it she forces back inside; some she takes to her desk. She doesn't know to zip up her backpack to prevent future spillage. The teacher announces it's language time. The other 29 students know, without being told, that this means they must take out their language duotang, a pen, and the novel they began reading yesterday. Annie sits there. She is caught up in her imagination, where she is up on stage with her favorite K-pop group. Everyone who has ever made fun of her will see the video on YouTube of her shining moment. They will fall all over themselves to apologize, to ingratiate themselves to her… *Tap, tap, tap!* The teacher raps on her desk to get Annie's attention and asks, "Annie, what should you have out in front of you?" Annie mumbles an apology and feels around in her desk. It is jammed full. When she eventually finds her novel, the cover is bent out of shape. She needs to be reminded about the duotang and pencil. During the lesson, Annie sits still and keeps her eyes toward the front. Although her body is in class, she's somewhere else in her imagination.
9:30 a.m.	Gino's teacher calls out to Miss G, "He can be part of this lesson." Miss G tells Gino to focus on the front, but he keeps trying to talk to Miss G. She shushes him and points to the teacher. The teacher asks the class if anyone knows the components of soil. Gino's eyes light up and Miss G whispers, "Raise your hand!" Gino does. His arm begins to wave. The teacher picks someone else. Gino's face falls. "But I have something important to say!" he calls out. The teacher tells him to wait his turn. She picks someone else to share their idea. Gino explodes: "I HAVE AN ANT FARM AT HOME!" Miss G tells him to apologize and explains that teachers don't pick everyone. Sometimes, we must keep our thoughts in our heads. Gino grumbles, loudly, "But I know all about soil!" "Why don't you tell me three things you know," Miss G says. Gino relaxes and quietly tells her some facts. She then prompts him to copy the notes on the board. He starts the first sentence and erases a few times. The letters don't look how he'd like them to. When Miss G tells him to copy the next sentence, he protests, "My hand hurts!" The bell is about to ring, so Miss G writes the rest for him. While she writes, Gino gets up out of his seat to check out the window. Still cloudy.	Annie's teacher tells the class to find groups for their science projects. They should be coming up with a hypothesis and dividing the work today. There's an experiment to conduct and document, charts and illustrations to create, and a presentation to prepare. Annie sits at her desk while her peers swarm into groups, calling across the room or making visual contact with friends to establish who belongs where. Annie tried to join a group once before, and ended up standing at the front, alone. She didn't know what to say or how to position her body so that peers would notice her. Since she thinks no one probably wants her in their group, she begins writing her hypothesis. Soon, her teacher notices she isn't with a group and asks Annie if she'd like to join Andrea's group. "I'd rather work by myself," Annie replies. "It's a lot of work if you're on your own," her teacher says. "Fine." "If that's what you really want, Annie."

10:00 a.m.	Miss G calls Gino back to his desk. "But it's snack time!" he protests. The teacher announces, "Please stay in your seats for a minute. I want to explain about the trip tomorrow before we get snacks." Gino looks at the clock. At 10:01, he makes his way to the bin and snatches his snack. Miss G and the teacher call to him in unison. He looks at Miss G and comes back to the desk, opening the snack and cramming the crackers into his mouth. The teacher dismisses the other rows, one at a time for snack. She picks Gino's row last, because "not everyone was listening." The kid in front of Gino turns around and glares at him. Gino doesn't know why. "He's bullying me!" he cries. Miss G tries to talk him down. Gino notices the time. He stops listening and makes his way to the window again.	Annie's teacher asks her if she'd like to hand out the snacks from the nutrition program. "No, thanks," says Annie, not realizing this is a request rather than a choice. The teacher asks someone else. Annie nibbles on the crackers but refuses the orange. The thought of it makes her gag.
Morning recess	Gino is late going out. He drags his heels and is the last one to the coat rack. He waits until everyone else has left. Miss G prompts him. He keeps glancing at the window. Finally, he gets an arm inside one sleeve. Then the other. It's hard to tell if it's reluctance or fine motor difficulties slowing him down. Probably both. It's still cloudy. By the time he gets outside, only five minutes remain. He steps out tentatively to find it isn't raining. He runs back and forth by the Kindergarten yard, flapping his arms and clinging to his Pokémon. He talks to it about ant farms. He is the last to line up to go back in, but pushes his way to the front of the line. The kid at the front protests and Gino protests right back, "I have to be first!"	Annie sits against the wall. She has brought out her binder of writing. She writes stories and her imagination is so vivid, she feels as though she can walk around inside of them. It is a 4-D experience. She doesn't notice anyone or anything else.
10:30 a.m.	In Gino's math class, he doesn't follow along while the teacher takes up the answers because his mom corrected it all at home. Miss G isn't there to tell him why it's important. Instead, he reads his favorite Pokémon book. He misses the lesson but at least he's quiet. During the work period, he calls out, "I don't know what to do!" The teacher comes over and tells him which questions to work on. "Is it the same as everyone else?" he asks. The teacher explains she gave him fewer questions and he insists, "I need to do all of it! I can do it!" When she walks away, he realizes he doesn't know where to start. The questions fall right out of his head. Miss G would normally write each question down on a sticky note and show them to him one by one. "Help me!" he calls out again. When the period is over, he has barely started. He keeps trying to write, saying, "Oh no, oh no, oh no, I'm not done!" As he becomes more anxious, his volume increases.	It's math time. Other Grade 7s take up the homework. Annie forgot all about the homework so doesn't have anything to review. She can't possibly look up each question and cross-reference with what's on the board, so she doesn't try. She is still and quiet, and no one notices she isn't following along. During the lesson, her teacher asks an easy question. The boy next to her gets it wrong. Annie raises her hand, perfectly straight. She gets picked! "Daryl was incorrect. It's 563, not 556," she states. The teacher confirms the answer. Annie turns to the boy and says, "Beat you!" Some kids laugh. Annie so rarely talks, they find this surprising. During the work period, Annie sings to herself in Korean. She doesn't notice the looks of classmates nearby. She doesn't regulate her volume. Finally, the boy next to her says, "Shut up!" Annie recoils out of her K-pop music fantasy and shoots him a withering look.

The Demands of School 13

10:30 a.m. (cont'd)	Finally, the teacher says, "If you don't stop, Gino, I'll have to tell your parents!" "Okay, okay, okay! Don't call them, please don't!" he repeats, putting down the pencil, eyes wide.	
11:00 a.m.	Miss G comes back to help Gino with the transition to gym. He doesn't want to leave. "No!' he says. Miss G asks him what's the matter. "She hasn't said she won't call them!" he replies. The teacher looks surprised and says, "Gino, I'm not going to call." "Promise?" "Yes. Just go to gym." Miss G prompts him to line up in his spot. "I can't find it!" he complains. "What number are you?" Miss G asks. "10!" "Why can't you find it?" "I lose count!" Miss G asks him who he is supposed to stand beside. "John and Kalim." "So, don't count. Look for them!" "Okay!" At gym, they're playing basketball. Gino puts his Pokémon on the bench. He dribbles low to the ground and slowly. He is usually on the fringes, trailing behind the others, ten seconds late to cheer or boo. When his team scores, he cheers and says, "In your face!" Most kids laugh, so he repeats it. He gets tired after a few minutes and daydreams on the spot. He wonders if Bulbasaur is watching him play. He is nearly hit by the ball when a peer misses a pass. "Gino!" someone calls and he startles, then chases after the ball with a huge grin, fumbling the pickup for a moment. He dribbles with both hands, travelling when he isn't supposed to. The kids know not to point it out. But one of the kids sees an easy target and steals the ball. "He did that on purpose!" says Gino. "It's part of the game," says the gym coach. When someone else scores, Gino gets teary-eyed. "No! I lost! I hate basketball!"	Annie goes to art class, collecting all her materials. Her pencil case opens (she never can manage the clasp) and everything inside spills over the floor. She is late to class, and blushes when all eyes turn toward her. Her teacher welcomes her and holds up her work for the class to see. Annie's heart races and she wishes she could turn invisible.
Lunch	Miss G gets Gino's lunch out for him since he is still upset about gym. She waits until he's eating, and calmer, before going on her own lunch. Gino tells the kids around him, "Be quiet" and "You're supposed to stay in your seats!" He threatens to tell their parents. Eating his lunch takes so long, he often stays behind with the lunch monitor to finish. He misses half of recess. Miss G catches him on his way out.	Annie doesn't eat. She isn't hungry. The boy next to her has tuna and the smell is overwhelming. Annie plugs her nose and says, "Your lunch stinks!" She waits until the bell rings and then gets her lunch— pretzels—out of her bag. She takes them with her to the Kindergarten class where she helps at lunch. She loves playing with the children and telling them what to do. She doesn't have to think hard about

14   *The Teacher/Student Disconnect*

Lunch (cont'd)	"Who are you going to play with?" she asks. "I don't know his name." Miss G guesses he means Chad, a sweet boy in his class. "I can't wait to hear all about it after recess!" she says. Gino shadows Chad and his friends as they move around the yard. Maybe they see him, maybe they don't. Gino gives up after a while and defaults to running by the fence, back and forth.	how to fit in or what words to say. Kindergarten is much easier. And the kids love her.
12:30 p.m.	Afternoons are always tough on Gino because he's tired. Today is worse. There's a supply teacher for French and no one told him. The supply teacher tells the class to settle down. Everyone gets louder when it's not their regular teacher. The teacher raises his voice and says, "Do you think I'm playing games here?" The class falls silent. Gino calls out, "We're not playing games, either!" "Do you think you're funny?" the supply teacher asks. Gino covers his ears. The teacher starts to reprimand him when Miss G walks in. She sits next to Gino, and the teacher recognizes he jumped to the wrong conclusion. "Sorry, buddy," he says. Miss G pulls Gino to finish the test from the day before he didn't complete. "No, it's too hard," Gino says. "You can do it, Gino." "Don't tell me what to do!" "You don't want to get a bad mark, do you?" "Just give me a 0!"	It's soccer in gym class. Annie shudders. She had a bad experience once when she worked up the courage to ask a group of girls to join. They said okay but then no one passed to her. She has avoided playing ever since, especially with those girls. The gym teacher asks Annie what position she wants. "None," Annie replies. "I want you to participate, Annie. Pick one." Annie freezes. There are no good options. "Goalie or forward?" Annie groans, teeth gritted like it's a life-or-death question. Finally, her teacher picks for her. "Forward. Get in there!" Annie walks, head down, into the game. She stands there unsure of what to do. The game goes on without her. Again.
Afternoon Recess	Gino takes his time getting ready. "But it might rain!" he calls out. The teacher tells him it won't. Miss G soothes him, distracting him with his Pokémon. "What are you and Bulbasaur going to do at recess?" They walk and talk until he's at the outside door. He sees how dark the sky is. "No!" He cries. "No!" "I don't know why you're upset," says Miss G. "Use your words!" Gino makes a guttural sound, falls to the floor to one side of the doorway, and buries his head under his arms. He is still there after all the classes come inside. His teacher tries to get him into class faster by saying, "Do we have to call your parents?" "NO!! YOU PROMISED!"	Annie's afternoon recess is the same as the morning one. The same as most days. She escapes into her writing and tunes out everything and everyone else. It begins to drizzle so she shuts her binder and imagines without it.

The Demands of School 15

2:00 p.m.	It takes the rest of the day to calm Gino down.	Annie forgets her binder outside and panics. She leaves the class without asking and the teacher calls after her, "You're supposed to ask permission!" "Sorry!" Annie says, hitting her head, "I'm so stupid." "It's okay. You can go." When Annie comes back, a writing prompt is on the board: *Where will you be in ten years?* She stares at the board and the paper. How does she know? How can she possibly answer? And because she can't, she doesn't. At the end of the period, her teacher asks who still needs to present to the class. Annie does, but she doesn't raise her hand. She stutters when she speaks in front of others. She hopes that if she doesn't say anything, her teacher won't notice.
2:45 p.m.	Miss G writes Gino's homework for him in his agenda, packs his bag, and helps him to put on his coat. He hugs her, holding on. "What a terrible day," he says, "I hate school." When they get outside, his mom asks for a full account of the day. Miss G fills her in. Gino hangs his head and clings to Bulbasaur. The last thing he wants is to relive this day again.	Annie doesn't write down the homework. It takes too long to do and she thinks she can remember it. She forgets two of the books she needs. The permission form for tomorrow's trip falls out of her bag and she doesn't notice in her rush out the door. She just wants to be home.

Unless you have an understanding of how the autistic brain is wired, it can be hard to spot all the challenges these students face each day at school or the very real communication breakdowns that can occur between teachers and students with autism. Annie and Gino worry me, for different reasons.

Annie's struggles are under the radar, so teachers might not recognize the many issues just below the surface. She does well academically but issues with socialization, organization, and anxiety will likely worsen with age. Like most students with autism, she has greater difficulty each year from about Grade 4 on, as the curriculum requires greater critical thinking, inferential thinking, and collaborative methods of learning (Garcia Winner, 2013). As with many females on the spectrum, as social nuances increase, she will be less successful at masking and may be at risk for mood disorders (Cai et al., 2018).

In comparison, Gino has more obvious needs and will probably always receive some form of support. He is also at risk for anxiety, depression, and suicidal ideation (Ashburner et al., 2010; Mayes et al., 2013b; Mukaddes & Fateh, 2010). Gino reminds me very much of a student who told me he wanted every day to be an 100% good day and his day would be completely ruined if it did not meet this exacting criteria. I can't even imagine if this was my benchmark for success. As with most teachers, I'm satisfied on any given day if I get through a third of my plans and no one goes to the hospital!

Let's break down some of the difficulties we saw in Annie's and Gino's day at school and where we'll learn more about each topic:

Social Issues (See Chapter 4)
- Not knowing how to interact with others

- Not knowing how to join others
- Either not aware of or misperceiving their impact on others
- Misperceiving intent of others
- Feeling or being bullied
- Social isolation
- Tendency to retreat into imagination as a coping mechanism
- Black-and-white thinking about friendships
- Interests not always age-appropriate or consistent with peers' interests
- Not knowing names of peers

Anxiety and Challenging Moments (See Chapters 6 and 7)

- Not being able to accurately predict reactions of others
- Significant phobias
- Difficulty letting go of past negative experiences
- Rigidity around the schedule, unexpected changes (e.g., supply teacher)
- Difficulty with transitions between subjects or classes
- Overly competitive, taking losses to heart
- Power struggles and large reactions in response to punishments or threats
- Fear of being singled out
- Perfectionism, such as erasing work and avoidance of difficult tasks, including not even trying if they think they can't do something well
- Fear of negative reports home
- Needing support to self-regulate and problem-solve

Organization (See Chapter 5)

- Physically losing materials or forgetting homework or assignments
- Difficulty with backpacks, pencil cases, and hidden rules about how to manage materials
- Missing group cues of when to take things out or put them away
- Trouble managing time and breaking down tasks on their own
- Lacking timeliness with deadlines, finishing lunches, tidying up

Hidden Rules (See Chapters 3 and 4)

- Blurting out
- Difficulty with not being picked to answer
- Not understanding why group activities or rules apply to them (e.g., taking up work)
- Incorrectly generalizing a rule based on one bad experience
- Misreading polite requests as real questions
- Pointing out mistakes of others or correcting others for minor infractions

Motor Skills & Coordination

- Difficulty with fine motor skills makes copying notes or writing in agenda laborious
- Difficulty with gross motor skills affecting participation in gym or recess games and causing embarrassment

Sensory Processing (See Chapter 6)

- Oversensitive to noises, smells, tastes, etc.
- Difficulty processing too much information at once
- Difficulty finding place in line amongst many moving bodies

The Demands of School 17

It's interesting to note that during the COVID-19 school shutdowns, many of my students thrived academically, though after several months of online learning they all reported that they missed school, especially peers. Their performance on school work improved because demands that were hard for them—interpreting social information, communicating face to face, peer interactions—were removed. Instead, they could work more at their own pace. Teachers delivered information in smaller chunks. Technology and visual aids were used. There was no need to assimilate and perform in one way.

Independence (See Chapters 5, 6, and 7)

- Prompt dependence
- Wanting to be treated the same as others, even when accommodations would level the playing field
- Reluctance (and not knowing how) to participate in group work
- Preferring to work alone

Communication (See Chapters 3 and 4)

- Literal thinking and lack of understanding of figurative language (e.g., rhetorical questions)
- Difficulty with open-ended tests
- Expecting adults to keep their word perfectly
- Bluntness and a lack of filtering thoughts that should be kept in their heads

My brother Danny's differences become a "disability" only when he is in settings that are not designed to support him. Figuring out under what conditions our autistic students thrive gives us a lot of information about how to design better classrooms. While you were reading the preceding section, you probably thought of some strategies you'd use in your classroom to help Annie or Gino. Maybe you felt overwhelmed at first glance, to see so many developing areas requiring support. You might have reflected on kids you've taught, and wished you'd had a better understanding of what was going on in their brains. Don't be hard on yourself. We don't do this job because it's easy! Language like "best practices" can make it seem like there's one right way to do something that will magically solve all your students' most challenging behaviors or struggles. But students and our relationship to them are complicated. What we see in September is just the tip of the iceberg. Depending on what we put in place, by June they might seem like a completely different child. But how do we know where to start?

I was lucky enough to collaborate with an exemplary teacher, Jasmine, for about five years. The first year, Jasmine felt inspired by my PD on autism and left wanting to make many changes to her own practice. She soon felt frustrated. How to accomplish it all? Never one to give up, she decided to pick one change to make at a time, slowly adding to or adjusting her practice. I now draw on this wisdom when I work with teachers. There is much we're already doing well; we do not need to reinvent the wheel. We choose what works for our unique classroom context. So when you don't know where to start, start with one thing.

I have chosen to use person-first terms like "student with autism" and identity-first terms like "autistic student" interchangeably. Person-first language is often touted by neurotypical people as a reminder to see the commonalities and the person regardless of their autism. Many people with autism prefer to call themselves autistic, as their unique brain wiring shapes how they think about and experience the world. I hope readers will see value in both perspectives.

A Note on Terminology

My students are wonderful children from Grades 4-8 who have autism and average to above-average cognitive and language abilities. This is often referred to as *high-functioning autism, Asperger Syndrome*, or, the current medical term, *autism level 1*. This book focuses on these learners on the autism spectrum, who are usually integrated in general classrooms.

Throughout the book, I have tried to steer clear of terms like *high-functioning* except where relevant to a study. Though still often used, this term is loaded with assumptions about the perceived level of intelligence or autism severity of an individual. Yet someone can score high on intelligence tests and struggle tremendously with daily life, or vice versa. This is probably why preferred terminology keeps changing; labels can never fully encapsulate the strengths and challenges of complex human beings.

The Boring Stuff

Let's get it out of the way. Let's cover some of the facts and figures that are important but less engaging than the rest of this book. As I sometimes say, I'm not a life-saving doctor, just the kind that can bore you to tears at a dinner party! Here's what we know—and don't know—about autism.

What is autism, anyway? That is the question! It's hard to nail down. What we know for sure is that autism is a complex, lifelong neurodevelopmental disorder (Public Health Agency of Canada, 2018). In North America, the current criteria for a diagnosis is laid out in the fifth edition of the *Diagnostic and Statistical Manual of Mental Disorders*, known as the DSM-V (American Psychiatric Association [APA], 2013). In brief, autism is characterized by significant impairments to communication and socialization, restricted patterns of interest or behaviors, and difficulties with other areas of functioning. Some individuals with autism might present with other co-morbid conditions, like intellectual disabilities, sleep disorders, language impairments, gastrointestinal issues, sensory processing difficulties, seizures, Tourette syndrome, ADHD, or anxiety (Public Health Agency of Canada, 2018; Smith & Samdup, 2018). Autism looks vastly different from person to person, which is why it is often referred to as a spectrum (Public Health Agency of Canada, 2018).

> My brother Danny was slow to talk and didn't show joint attention or respond to verbal prompts. His hearing was tested more than once and he spent many sessions with a speech pathologist as my parents tried to figure out why. Although there weren't earlier signs, Danny's brain had already begun its unique pattern of arranging and wiring itself, starting when he was in utero.

Autism starts, well, at the beginning. In the first trimester, a fetus (who may one day be diagnosed with autism) is developing and organizing its brain in an unusual way, resulting in developmental differences that show up later on (Beversdorf et al., 2005, as cited in Smith & Samdup, 2018). There aren't reliable biological markers yet, so doctors diagnose autism based on behavioral symptoms. You can't look at a newborn and tell, because all babies are born looking pretty similar—their eyes don't usually focus, and they sleep and cry a lot. By 6 to 12 months of age, babies are expected to display certain milestones. This is when the trained eye might first notice that babies who will later be diagnosed with autism are not developing along a neurotypical pathway. Children with autism can be reliably identified by age two (Smith & Samdup, 2018), though most are diagnosed after age four (Baio et al., 2018).

After birth, the brains of autistic children begin growing rapidly, so that when they are about four years old, their brains are close to maximum volume, a stage their peers won't reach for another eight years (Courchesne et al., 2003). This overgrowth comes at the expense of neural connections. Autistic children tend to have strong clusters of brain connections in localized areas, but areas of the brain that are farther apart do not develop the pathways that connect strongly to one another (Vermeulen, 2012). I've always found this interesting, because every autism deficit seems to me to be a problem with connection. Connecting to others; connecting the right expectations to the context; connecting the right meaning to words or figurative language; connecting cause and effect; connecting and integrating many skills when approaching complex tasks… I could go on! It's also the challenge of those around them to connect to autistic folks and to imagine, as best we can, how much harder our lives would be if all types of connections were not intuitive and often unconscious processes.

> Sometimes, people ask me about the "vaccines cause autism" myth, caused by a faulty research study using falsified data. It has been retracted, and many other peer-reviewed, large scale studies have disproved its findings (Chen et al., 2004; Hviid et al., 2019; Taylor et al., 2014). While vaccines can cause side effects in some cases, autism is NOT one of them.

No one knows all the possible causes of autism. What research overwhelmingly shows is that genetics are involved. Autism tends to run in families. I can look across my family and see one or two brilliant thinkers who might qualify for a diagnosis today that wasn't available or needed when they were growing up. I have a couple of cousins with Asperger Syndrome. I consider myself more neurodivergent than neurotypical, though I do not have an autism diagnosis. Hundreds of genes, of all kinds, have been identified that can make a person more likely to display autism symptoms (Ansel et al., 2017).

Now, I vaguely recall learning in high school biology that not all genes are expressed. It's the same with autism. Genes can also be activated by certain epigenetic triggers, such as environmental factors in utero, and researchers continue to study these (Smith & Samdup, 2018). There's also a gender difference. Autism is diagnosed four to five times more often in males than in females (Baio et al., 2018; Public Health Agency of Canada, 2018; Smith & Samdup, 2018), and females who are diagnosed tend to have many more genetic mutations or differences than males (Jacquemont, 2014). In other words, autism susceptibility genes might be there, but fewer of these are required for autism to be expressed in males. It's also possible we just aren't as good at diagnosing autism in girls. Current diagnostic tests are based on male behaviors, and girls, especially those without intellectual delays, are better at masking their symptoms (Attwood, 2007; Cook et al., 2018). Recently in Australia, researchers developed a screener to identify more females on the spectrum, though this tool is still being validated (Ormond et al., 2018). We also know there is tremendous gender and sexual diversity across the spectrum, and more research is needed to consider autistic experiences in all folks.

> I suspect in my lifetime there will be considerable change to our understanding of autism and how we diagnose it.

Autism seems to be everywhere these days. Maybe it's because social media curates my experiences, but TV shows, movies, and articles about autism abound, and many more memoirs and perspectives are available from autistic people than when Danny was growing up. In North America, autism is estimated to be as common as 1 in 36 to 1 in 68 (Baio et al., 2018; Blumberg et al., 2013; Public Health Agency of Canada, 2018; Xu et al., 2018). That means, at least every few years, teachers will have a student with autism in their class.

We also don't have exact answers for why autism rates have risen over the last 30 years. It could be we're getting better at diagnosing kids. Rates of learning disabilities and intellectual disabilities have decreased, so we may also be shifting people from one category to another (Shattuck, 2006). It could be society is more aware of the signs of autism, so parents know what to bring up to doctors. One of the most probable reasons that autism seems to be increasing is that we've broadened the definition. In 1995, Asperger Syndrome was added as a possible diagnosis, allowing people with no intellectual delay to be diagnosed with autism for the first time in North America. Doctors had a whole new category to consider. Since 46% of people on the spectrum have average to above-average intelligence, that's a lot of folks who were previously missed (ADDMN Surveillance Year 2010 Principal Investigators, 2014). In the version of the DSM released by the APA in 2013, distinct categories of autism like Asperger were removed in favor of a general autism diagnosis and specified level of support. As we learn and expand our thinking about autism, this definition might continue to change.

Still, we're still not catching everyone. Autism is under-diagnosed in rural and lower socioeconomic areas and in Black or Latinx children in North America (Antezana et al., 2017; Baio et al., 2018). Other barriers exist, such as long wait lists for assessments through schools and the high cost of private assessments. Cultural stigma also plays a part, as autism may be considered taboo, a Western phenomenon, or simply "bad behavior," which could also affect rates of diagnosis. Diagnostic tools have not yet been developed to be relevant to all demographics, and so questions might reflect a significant bias. For instance, a typical screening question might ask about how a child lines up their toys, assuming a child has many toys to line up in the first place! It's also important to note that Western cultural norms value certain behaviors, such as independence, competition, and outgoing interpersonal skills; individuals who fall outside of those margins could be seen through a deficit lens in that context. It's entirely possible they would not need a diagnosis somewhere else, where other qualities are valued.

You may have realized, by now, that I lied about this being boring. I find this stuff endlessly fascinating! One of the factoids I like to tell my students is that genetic researchers discovered that early modern humans evolved to have different kinds of brains, whereas Neanderthals did not. They speculate that diverse minds, including those with autism and ADHD, allowed the human species to innovate and survive, while those without neurodiversity failed to thrive and eventually became extinct (Weiss, 2015). I can still hear one group of students cheering, "WE'RE IN THE ONE PERCENT!"—their statistic, not mine! It's important to remember, regardless of definition, that autistic people have always been here; it's just that we have not always looked at people's behavior through a microscope the way we do today.

One of the hardest parts of conversations about autism is that needs vary widely across the spectrum. For some, autism presents incredible barriers to a fulfilling life for people with autism and their families. These families may be desperate for support and may wish for a "cure." For others, autism comes with gifts and is just another way of being and thinking; while there can be significant challenges for these folks, they are more likely to reject interventions that aim to dull uniqueness and that require conformity. My goal in working with families is to help them—and their children—to know that autistic ways of thinking and being are as valid and worthy as "neurotypical" ways. Receiving a diagnosis isn't always clear cut, and families may not know how independent, social, or successful their child could be one day. It is a process riddled with anxiety, and families need our support and understanding. No matter where families and individuals are on their journey, as teachers we can play a powerful role in improving their quality of life. We can also help peers to become more compassionate—a step toward a more empathetic, less judgmental society.

As teachers, we're sometimes the first to notice that children are developing differently from their peers. Children I work with, who have autism and average to above-average intelligence and language skills, are more likely to be diagnosed much later than those with intellectual delays and autism (Christensen, 2016; Safran, 2008; Shepherd & Waddell, 2015). This is a disadvantage, as research is brimming with the benefits of early intervention (Clark et al., 2018; Matson & Konst, 2013; Smith & Samdup, 2018), and we know that high IQ doesn't always mean the person will have adaptive skills they need to succeed (Clark et al., 2018). This is not to say that any child with autism can't succeed or won't. They simply need our help, and we need to know what to really look for. It also means that it often falls to teachers to bridge the gap in services for students with autism who can keep up with grade-level work. We have to understand more than the textbook definition of autism. We have to understand what challenges our students might experience in the classroom and how to mitigate them.

Let's pretend, for a moment, that I didn't give you all that background. Here's the description of autism I much prefer to all the clinical stuff, from someone who knows what they're talking about (and who would be the most interesting person to talk to at a dinner party!). In the words of my student Amanda, "Autism is when everyone else wants cotton candy and all you want is a grape."

The Boring Stuff 21

2

Connecting Your Worldview to Theirs

Communication Breakdown

In class, he is trying his best to copy what's on the blackboard. He grips the pencil tightly, hand shaking from enormous concentration. He stands and approaches the board. He wants to get it down perfectly, and there's only a minute left before the bell. Voices erupt: "Sit down!" and "You're blocking my view!"

He doesn't realize, at first, that they are talking to him. He doesn't turn to look. "You're so rude, Colin!" "What a jerk!"

He startles. There they go again, picking on him. As usual. For no reason!

At recess, he joins a game of tag. He's fast and doesn't mind being It, so long as he gets to play. As he gains on the other kids, they react in anger, recoiling. Someone swears at him. He has no idea why. Why does no one like him? When he gets home, he sobs until he can't breathe.

When Colin came to see me the next day, he told me about being bullied. His distress was palpable. I empathized and asked for the details so we could problem-solve what to do next. I realized quickly that Colin wasn't seeing what his peers were seeing. In class, when he inadvertently blocked the blackboard, he heard only the frustrated tones of peers and didn't connect these to his own actions. Nor were peers aware of Colin's intentions and thought process. How could I help him to see?

I drew a quick comic of what it must look like to his peers. He filled in thought bubbles over their heads. We talked about whether peers gave him any useful feedback, even if they were doing it in a rude way. Sometimes, there's still a message that we can learn and grow from.

"Oh," Colin said, "Maybe I could've stood to the side."

"Next time!" I said. "Now, tell me about what happened in your game of tag."

Colin re-enacted it, his hand oddly curled into a fist with his thumb emerging between his pointer and index fingers. I probed, "Wait, why were you holding your hand like that?"

"I had my house keys!"

"Hmm. I wonder what the other kids were thinking when you ran at them with a piece of metal between your fingers?" I acted it out, lunging at him in slow motion.

"Oh, my goodness!" He began to laugh. "Yeah, I guess that would be kinda scary."

"Probably!" I probed some more, "Now, why were you holding your keys?"

"I was afraid to lose them."

With that information, we could problem-solve. What do others do with their keys to keep them safe? When is he more likely to lose his keys: when he has them playing at recess or when they're tucked away in his backpack? Where would he feel is the safest place to keep them?

Like all my students, to varying degrees, Colin needs explanations to understand how others see the world. He perceives all situations from his unique worldview. He is only beginning to learn that others also see from their individual vantage points. When each puzzling situation is freeze-framed and analyzed, he can process all the information. It's not so overwhelming as it is in real time. When we hit the pause button, he can expand his perspective. It's in these moments that I also broaden my own.

An Invisible Disability

Recently, my class was playing Two Truths and a Lie, the game in which each person states three facts and the group tries to guess which statement is not true. Pedro declared three remarkably similar facts: *I like the color green. I like the color purple. I like the color red.* When he finally revealed he didn't like red, he looked at the floor and said, "Every day in Kindergarten, a note went home with a red frowny face. I don't know why. I could never get the green smiley."

Twelve years old, and he still hates the color red! Pedro and some of my other students get in trouble all the time for things they usually can't help. While others in the class can usually figure out why a teacher is suddenly serious or angry, my kids really don't know. They will tattle or call out, right after a whole-class lecture on not doing those things. They will answer a rhetorical question or point out a spelling mistake when a teacher is clearly having a bad day. They don't know what they're doing wrong and they don't know how not to get into trouble. They just can't figure out other people. And it stays with them, because they want to do well. They want the green smiley. They just don't know what they have to do to get one.

One of the practices I implemented in my classes is to allow students to write in their journals questions they want answers to. It gives me insights into what they are wondering about and I am not pressed to respond on the spot. This allows me to write a thoughtful response or plan what to say when I next conference with them. Pedro's first entry read: *I want to know if there is a way for people to be calmer with me and stop yelling.* For his entire life, Pedro will probably be the smartest person in the room. He is curious about everything and makes brilliant connections. His constant questions can sound like he's playing devil's advocate. He sounds and looks argumentative, but his intention is to understand.

Unfortunately, he feels adults are always yelling at him. After reading his journal, we sat together and I explained how sometimes the message we send comes from our face and bodies, and less from our words: "For instance, right now you look angry."

"This is my thinking face!"

"I know! However, your thinking face looks the same as your angry face. Your mouth puckers into a grimace, your jaw is tense, and your eyebrows make train tracks."

We walked to the mirror to practice how to make his eyebrows appear more sympathetic. If I'd filmed it, you would see the visible strain required for Pedro to soften his eyebrow furrow, even a little.

"Too much," I said, as his eyebrows lifted off his head, eyes bulging. "That looks angry again."

"It's so hard!" he exclaimed.

I explained he might want to practice in the mirror before making requests to parents or teachers, especially important ones. He shook his head, possibly frowning at his angry eyebrows, or possibly thinking deeply.

"So, that's why people are always reacting to me badly."

My students have an invisible disability. You can't look at them and see their struggles. You can see what they understand, but miss all the gaps. After all, their strengths can be dazzling. They are artists, mathematicians, scientists, computer whizzes, linguists, and more. They spend so much time engaging in their interests, it's no wonder they become authorities on these topics, possessing expertise far beyond their peers (Attwood, 2007). They are often bright and interesting to talk to. They are passionate about their ideas and so, if those ideas happen to align with what you're teaching, it's a joy to watch their learning unfold and to learn in the process. Children with high-functioning autism can speak about and engage in their special interests excessively without paying attention to the interests or interest level of those around them (Berenguer et al., 2018). However, if what we're teaching is hard for them or not a preference, academic difficulties begin to surface. Our current education system does not allow kids to specialize in their interests. It's designed to teach them a bit of everything, broadly, so they can eventually narrow down to specific areas that could one day become their career path. It makes sense. But kids with autism already have the specialties and are being asked to devote time to tasks that they do not understand or do not need in order to be successful in their areas of expertise. I imagine I'd feel the same if you pulled me out of my elementary classroom and dropped me in Chemistry 100; I'd be completely out of my element.

I'm not advocating for a curricular overhaul. Kids with autism and without intellectual impairments can access the curriculum, but might need teachers who understand how they think, and how they approach the work and the world. Ideally we should recognize how hard they are working as they spend tons of brainpower figuring out social communication that surrounds them at school *in addition* to the regular work. We must teach them, step by step, what is harder for them than for others, or why something might be important for them to do, even if they find it boring. The problem is, because we see how brilliantly they handle some tasks, we often assume that other tasks should be easy for them. Their cognitive and verbal strengths mask their disability (McCrimmon et al., 2012; Safran & Safran, 2001; Stichter et al., 2010). At a glance, we can't always see how their diagnosis significantly affects their learning, socialization, and emotional well-being. Don't be discouraged. Research shows that students with autism can be successful in classrooms if teachers know what to tweak to support their growth and understanding across domains.

Challenges in Perspective-Taking

Human beings without autism are hardwired to process social information in the blink of an eye. It's easy to forget how incredibly complex social communication is! We are constantly sending and receiving hidden social messages that our students with autism are not privy to. I prefer face-to-face conversations so I can assess how my message is being received and adjust as necessary; however, my brother Danny fares better with digital communication that he can interpret at his own pace and on a literal level without the layers of ambiguity that make sense to me. There is no need for him to read faces, look at eyes, or process anything other than the text. I see the forest; he sees a tree.

To people with autism, the thoughts of others are elusive. They struggle with theory of mind (Baron-Cohen, 1995), the ability to figure out what other people are thinking, feeling, or wanting, and to use that information to make sense of the actions and predict future behaviors of others. Some children with autism may not yet be aware that others even have thoughts. If they are aware, they might assume everyone possesses the same information they do and therefore thinks the same way. They may misread intent, like my student Dwayne, who accused the peacocks at the zoo of purposefully interrupting our picnic, or Tim, who thought his baby brother was crying to make him fail his test—*Why's he doing that? It must be on purpose! That jerk!*

Even knowing about difficulties with theory of mind, I am sometimes caught off-guard by how my students react to situations everyone else just seems to get. A few years ago, a local toddler died after wandering outside on a freezing winter night. The tragedy was all over the news and our community was grief-stricken. After a tear-filled school assembly, my student David asked me why it was such a big deal.

"Sorry?" I blinked.

"Why's everyone so upset? He wanted to die."

"No, David, he didn't."

"He was clearly trying to commit suicide. Why else would he go out with no jacket in a snowstorm?"

"David, toddlers don't have the same knowledge you and I have. He didn't know what would happen. Babies and toddlers haven't learned what is and isn't dangerous yet. They don't know they can get hurt or die. It was a terrible accident."

David blanched as the weight of the tragedy landed.

It got me thinking about empathy. If I hadn't explored David's thinking, I could have easily written him off as callous. Later, as I listened to a TEDtalk by Simon Baron-Cohen (2012) on the two parts of empathy, it clicked. People with autism struggle with cognitive empathy, the perspective-taking piece. However, if they have experienced the situation before or if someone takes the time to explain the perspective, they are able to show affective empathy, demonstrating an appropriate empathetic response. So if a response isn't what you'd expect from one of your students, it's worth considering *What aren't they understanding?*

Part and parcel of perspective-taking challenges is difficulty reading the emotional states of others. Students with autism might be able to distinguish the basic emotions in others, like happiness or anger, but nuanced expressions are harder to read (Attwood, 2007; Vermeulen, 2012). Of course, noticing subtle changes in faces requires looking. Most of us unconsciously process the huge amount of social information going on around us. Our eyes and brains know what to do. My students don't always understand what to do with their eyes and they aren't aware how much eyes communicate the thoughts, feelings, and intentions of others. For their whole lives, they may have been missing out on the social information conveyed through eyes.

One of the early signs that an infant or toddler could have autism is the lack of developing the milestone of joint attention (Elder et al., 2008). When watching movies, children with autism have been found to focus their attention in unpredictable patterns, while their more typically developing peers consistently attend to relevant social information, such as eyes, facial expression, and gesture (Avni et al., 2019). If we think about it, it's not just faces that we use to convey our feelings—it's gesture, eye gaze, tone of voice, what is said, what is not said… Perhaps people with autism just don't know what's important to look for! When directed to specifically look for emotions and context clues in a photo or movie clip, they tend to have an easier time identifying relevant social information (Vermeulen, 2012). In real-life interactions, expressions change from second to second and there is so much going on all around them they can't intuitively attend to context clues. When they do identify someone's feelings, it is significantly harder for them to figure out why the person might be feeling that way. That's theory of mind, or perspective-taking.

People with autism are routinely disadvantaged by social norms that prioritize eye contact and nonverbal communication. They report that eye contact can be physically painful or impossible to maintain when they also have to process auditory information (Grandin, 2006; Hadjikhani et al., 2017). Unfortunately, people without autism make a lot of assumptions about others based on their nonverbal cues. For instance, we are likely to assume someone is listening when they are looking at us and we deem them rude if they do not. Little do we know it might be causing them distress to do so!

My heart broke once when I walked into a school where my student John was in trouble for yelling in class and, eventually, flipping a desk. In the aftermath of the incident, one of the school staff demanded he look at her while she lectured him on the seriousness of his behavior, and I could see he was becoming more and more agitated. The intended message was not registering, and his not living up to the expectation of eye contact was making the situation worse. After I introduced myself, the staff was happy to let me intervene. I told John he could sit down and take deep breaths for a moment. Then I lowered my voice to ask him what had got him so upset. It turned out he had won a major award outside of school and had been promised it would be announced over the PA system. Morning announcements came and went without the expected acknowledgment. He probably showed some agitation. He may have whined, "It's not fair!" When he didn't feel heard, the whining turned into yelling until finally… *Boom!* His desk avalanched to the floor. John—like many of us—could calm down only after feeling someone understood his personal crisis. Then, with a more level head, he could talk with me about what choices might have resulted in a better outcome for him, and the repair process could begin.

I teach my students two potential strategies for situations when eye contact is someone's expectation, depending on their comfort level. First, they can self-advocate by saying they can't always look and listen at the same time. Secondly,

26   *Connecting Your Worldview to Theirs*

they can cheat by looking at the bridge of the person's nose. It's impossible to tell the difference between that and eye contact! I also spend time teaching them other "listening look-fors" in the classroom, so they can understand that their bodies convey information about their state of mind, whether they intend them to or not.

Listening Look-Fors

Once, I observed another student in his classroom. The teacher was in the middle of introducing fractions, and Dwayne was out of his seat with his hands in the bins, grabbing glue and scissors. His back was fully to the teacher. I beckoned him over.

"Does your teacher think you're listening?"

"Well, I *am*!"

"Does she *think* you're listening? Are you showing any of the look-fors? Is your body doing what your classmates are doing?"

"Huh! Nope, not at all!"

At other times, neurotypical folks must seem like mind-readers to those with autism. I've had to explain that teachers everywhere can usually tell that they're daydreaming by tracking their eye gaze. Once, at parents' night, a father of one of my students blurted, "How do you do that? Any time I'm about to contribute, you're already looking at me!" He had no idea that I turned to face him in response to the many clues that he gave that he was about to speak—a deep inhale, a slight movement forward, sitting up straight, eyes lifted from the table to the group. For me, it was simple.

For those who are good at all this social stuff, it's amazing the conclusions we jump to in our thinking about autistic students. *Why's he doing that? It must be on purpose! He doesn't care!* In reality, we're experiencing the same thing our students do: sheer bewilderment at someone else's behavior and a desperate need for an explanation to make sense of it! The communication breakdown occurs on both sides.

This is where our autism lens comes in. Knowing what I now know about the autistic brain and its neurological difficulties with theory of mind, it makes sense that the responsibility to change perspective starts with me. Using my autism lens has made me more patient, kinder, and better able to pinpoint the source of misunderstandings. It has helped me to check my instinct to jump to conclusions. And dealing with autistic students no longer feels like an endless sequence of trial and error. If I don't know what they're thinking or why, I ask them. The beauty is, by perspective-taking ourselves, we can better plan what and how to teach them to develop their own perspective-taking.

Literal Thinking

Sonia and I went to observe David in his classroom, arriving at his portable just as the class was beginning daily physical activity. "Reach for the ceiling," the teacher called out. David was the only one who got on a chair, fingers desperately straining to touch the roof. Sharing a glance, Sonia and I immediately recognized what had happened.

Our students tend to interpret information at face value. They do not always understand flexible uses of language, such as figurative language or sarcasm

(Attwood, 2007). They will physically grab a partner instead of finding one the usual way. They'll ask, "Where should I put it?" when directed to take a seat. When a teacher makes a polite request like, "Do you mind handing this out, please?" they'll refuse, believing the teacher is truly seeking their opinion. I am more and more aware of how vague and unpredictable the language we use is, and just how much we communicate through nonverbal cues instead. Sarah, a student in Grade 8, told me one of her biggest challenges is not having access to technology at school, because people frequently use idioms she recognizes as figures of speech, but can't discern their meaning. She expends an enormous amount of energy trying to remember these to look up when she gets home! It makes me wonder how much she is missing while she is trying to process vague parts of a sentence. The endless stream of information in a classroom waits for no one!

People with autism can have trouble with idioms, taking them literally.

This literal thinking also means people with autism may be unable to pick up on deception (Attwood, 2007; Baron-Cohen, 1992, as cited by Gedek et al., 2018). My students are usually able to perceive deception in movies or TV shows, especially when expressions are exaggerated, but are not so good in real life with peers who are sometimes nice to them and at other times trying to convince them to go hug the most popular girl in the class and tell her that they want to marry her. I've had two students, both around 13, who did not realize that everything they'd seen in movies was not real. I had to pull up a movie database and show them the main actors in various roles. *Look: there is Patrick Stewart as Professor Xavier. There he is as Captain Picard, walking around the USS Enterprise. No wheelchair!* We searched for clips of movies being filmed, so the students could see all the crew behind the scenes. I talked about the thousands of people working on a major motion picture—script writers, directors, foley artists, special effects, hair and makeup, you name it. One student was incredibly relieved to learn it was all staged, as he'd been horrified that so many people he knew were entertained by what he took to be real people killed or injured in action movies!

It is interesting to note that many of my students can pick up on insincerity in adults and have a preference for adults who truly like them!

The other student walked around for the next few months as if he were in *The Truman Show*, questioning the heavens: *What else in my life isn't real?* Because of their age and average academic performance, no one had thought to mention to them that movies aren't real.

Literal thinking can translate into steadfast adherence to rules. It makes sense to me that if the whole world was confusing and unpredictable, I'd cling to the things in life that made sense and were easy to predict. Clinically speaking, this is rigidity, a feature of autism. My students sometimes annoy peers by being quick to notice everyone else's shortcomings but not seeing their own. They're the kids blurting out to complain that someone else interrupted. They get upset with teachers who fall behind in the schedule or forget about snack time. Those are the rules that make sense to them and they expect everyone else to see things in black and white, too. Being right at all costs seems more important than smoothing things over for the sake of social relationships. I like to call them members of their very own justice league.

Their justice priorities usually have to do with being perceived accurately. Two of my students, Jeffrey and Ryan, were bickering on the walk to a nearby pizzeria for a group outing. I was chatting with another kid when I heard Ryan complain, "Ms. Dymond, Jeffrey said he wants to crush my bones!" As I turned to face Jeffrey, he piped up, "No, I didn't say that! What I *actually* said was that I wanted to crush his hopes and dreams!" I blinked and controlled my face for a moment, appreciating his creativity, before saying, "Is that really better?" What struck me was how Jeffrey couldn't stand being misreported. On the spot, it didn't occur to him to deny the accusation (and if it had, it would have been utterly transparent, like the time he denied eating his classmate's chocolate, despite the evidence lining his mouth). Guile isn't natural or habitual to him, or to most of my students. It's usually easy to get to the bottom of things. If only all kids were as honest!

People with autism can have trouble understanding that there's such as thing as too much honesty. They don't always see why they can't say everything they think, feel, or observe. Someone is overweight—why not point it out? Surely, they're aware they're overweight! Mom's haircut is ugly—tell her immediately so she can fix it. Someone is stupid—that's not an insult; it's the truth! As annoying as it might be to everyone else, they can mistake their opinion for objective fact, acknowledged by all. While I admit it would be remarkably freeing to say everything I think, I'd be in a world of trouble most of the time if I did. Instead, I am fortunate to have the social processing power to wrap my messages to others in the wrapping I think they'll best respond to (and the know-how to keep my gifts of wisdom to myself when they are not helpful). My students don't notice how others do this, so they don't do it themselves.

What literal thinking gives my students is a beautiful sense of logic, like the time I went to play a video and Ryan informed me the mute button was on.

"Where would I be without you?" said I.

"Well, without volume!" said he, with a smile.

Many of my students, and my brother Danny, possess a profound wit, often based on logic and wordplay. They approach tasks and think about the world in a way that is different from that of many of their peers and teachers. They make exciting connections that help everyone else think more deeply about topics. Sometimes this is embraced, and sometimes it isn't. It is so much more enjoyable for everyone if we can appreciate it and be enlightened!

Challenges in Perspective-Taking 29

> ### Innovative Insights
>
> Pedro once wrote a persuasive essay on all the ways school is like jail. I'm not sure how it went over at his home school, but I laughed and told him he made some great connections.
>
> > Classrooms are like cells. You are always guarded by someone. Uniforms. Your gym and recess are short, structured, and you don't have much choice. Everything occurs at set times. If you do something wrong, you are punished by adding time to your sentence (detention).
>
> The list went on. I asked him and his classmates if they could also debate the other side and think from a different perspective. What is good about school? A chorus of voices called out, "March Break!" "Summer vacations!" "Weekends!" "Extracurricular activities!"
>
> Pedro grinned ear to ear and quipped, "So, basically, the best parts about school are all related to when we get to leave it. In conclusion, school equals jail."

Through their questions and comments, people with autism often hold up a mirror so we can examine ourselves. Have we been clear enough? Can we laugh at ourselves? Do we seek to understand them? Are we someone who is safe to share with, and who may appreciate their insights?

Everything is easier if we can answer yes!

Strategies to Build Perspective-Taking

As a classroom teacher, you can support students' developing perspective-taking abilities throughout the day. As with any students learning any skill, students with autism benefit from direct instruction, practice, and slowing down the stream of social information.

- Across subjects, help them to understand that others see things differently by thinking out loud to model how you come to an answer or approach a task.
- Use clear language and explain figures of speech.
- Show exemplars or the process. Use a document camera to help you demonstrate what you mean while you talk through each scenario.
- Give the class chances to see there is more than one acceptable way to answer a question: "Would anyone approach this differently?" "What might be a different opinion?"
- Seek opinions without overt corrections or reacting negatively to the sharing of an autistic student. If someone's thinking is not the direction I hoped to take, I will sometimes say, "That wasn't how I was thinking about it," "I'm not sure about that," or "What you've said makes me wonder…" and build upon the point. When possible, validate their thinking: "Amanda brings up a great point!"

See page 35 for a template for possible Tickets Out the Door.

- Seek opinions through different modalities, such as a journal or a Ticket Out the Door, to encourage quieter students to share. Use their feedback to inform your next lesson or to revisit a favorite activity, and then let students know that the reason you've done this is because you valued their opinions. They will be happy to share their opinions this way in future when they see it has an impact on the classroom!
- Help them to see that others have perspectives of their own and all are welcome to share in your classroom. Students with autism sometimes get stuck on not being picked to share an answer. Explain how you equitably try to give different students a chance, but that you notice their hand up. Some students

benefit from having an ideas journal or clipboard to write down what they wish to say and share later. If another student arrives at an answer first, a student with autism may protest that they stole their idea. Congratulate them both on having the same great idea!

- Survey students in your class when an answer or opinion is shared so that more students feel like they are participating in valuable ways: "How many people in the class feel the same as Ryan?"
- If students with autism dislike an activity or assignment, explain the purpose and ask them if they have ideas to improve the assignment or show their knowledge another way.
- Accept and show exemplars of different types of responses, such as comics, role plays, debates, diagrams combined with short written responses, etc. If you have made your task criteria clear and provided a rubric, students should be able to understand what it is you are looking for. Prompt students to look over their work from your point of view: "Did you compare your product with the rubric?" "Have you double-checked that you met all my criteria?" It sometimes helps to remind them that, since you are the person marking the work, you give them feedback to help them to meet your expectations so they can learn as much as possible and potentially get a better mark.

Short, Engaging Activities

- Experiment with a variety of mindfulness activities and ask students to share (if they wish) how they are feeling and which activities they prefer. I have found guided meditations, in which students explore highly imaginative landscapes and are given time to imagine without interruption, promote student motivation and visualization abilities. In the beginning, I prompt students to imagine my words happening as if they are seeing a movie in their mind. After a mindfulness activity, students are invited to share what they imagined and we celebrate how everyone thinks and feels differently. I now use the movie-in-your-mind prompt before read-alouds and have observed a significant increase in attention and engagement.
- Consider having a daily or weekly perspective-taking activity for the class that does not have a right or wrong answer, so that students can come to appreciate that we can think flexibly. I sometimes pull up abstract images or inkblots and have students write down what they see before volunteers can share their answers. Students are challenged to try to see it someone else's way! You could also project a picture of a painting or photograph and give students a writing or discussion prompt. What might the character be thinking or feeling? What is written in the letter they are reading? What might happen next?
- Have class board games, such as Apples to Apples Junior or Bubbletalk, that promote perspective-taking abilities. These can be played during indoor recess or adapted as a whole-class warm-up where the teacher picks a card or two and the class votes on three possible answers.

Language, Social Studies, and the Arts

- Read aloud from books and ask students questions that prompt them to infer characters' thoughts, feelings, and intentions. Draw attention to the clues in the text that are important to figure this out. Ask students to predict or suggest how a character might react next, or another possible reaction or choice they

Strategies to Build Perspective-Taking 31

Language, social studies, and the arts are natural subjects to promote students' thinking about the thoughts and feelings of others in a variety of contexts. When planning these lessons, ask yourself whether you have built in opportunities to perspective-take.

could have made. You might wish to ask them to personally connect to a time they'd felt similarly or what advice they would give the character. Questions should focus on developing critical thinking and perspective-taking.

- Explicitly teach about author intent, audience, and other concepts that seem obvious to most adults but might not be to students with autism! Ask them to consider what an author or producer intended audiences to understand after reading or showing different media texts. The more practice they have, the easier this will become for them to do!

- Literature circles can help students approach texts from a variety of angles and can be highly structured. For each chapter, students can rotate through roles, which may include producing a response as a cartoonist, rewriting text to reflect a different choice, writing a first-person diary of a character, developing conversation starters for the group, making a movie trailer for the chapter, summarizing the chapter in a timeline, etc.

- Choose writing tasks that prioritize writing from the perspectives of others to enrich student understanding of concepts. Show exemplars so that students understand what is expected of them and consider offering a range of options from structured to less-structured. Perspective-taking writing can begin early and can be fun for the whole class.

In a Grade 1 science unit, I had the class come up with structure riddles: each student pretended to be a household object and had to give clues so we could guess what they were (e.g., "I am solid, found near a table, and people sit on me"). Combining media, structures, and animal research projects, they also wrote short House Wanted ads for different animals, reflecting their specific needs (e.g., "Home with high ceilings needed. Must have trees and water on property. Bedrooms not important since we can sleep standing up, and only for 20 minutes a day. Please contact Mrs. Giraffe").

- Art is all about perspective: both visual spatial skills and what the artist and audience perceive. Have these conversations. Encourage students to share what they see when they look at art, or what they were trying to convey as an artist.

- Music expresses emotions! Students can identify the mood of music through words or movement, or by free writing a story to match what they hear. They can develop soundscapes that require perspective-taking (e.g., to convey a theme park: what sounds need to be included to tell the story?)

Practice Makes Perfect

Before I began teaching, I developed a drama program for kids with autism. Drama is a natural vehicle to experiment with perspective, choices, emotions, reactions, and much more. As a director, I could freeze scenes and ask the audience to make predictions or interpret what an actor was trying to show. I would ask audience members to share how they specifically knew a character was, say, angry: What was it about what their body or voice was doing that showed that? I could also redirect to make something clearer, helping actors to connect more with their faces, bodies, and tones of voice. It gave me a real-time glimpse of social understanding. You can also ask these questions while viewing movies or video clips.

Science, Health, and Math

- Talking through your process and showing how to approach problems can help students with autism understand how to explain their own steps. Often, my students can get to an answer very quickly but can't perspective-take to be able to explain what they did. Practice with the whole class explaining their thinking on math problems or when developing a hypothesis, which require an awareness of audience that may not come naturally to students with autism!

- Ask the class to suggest how concepts might help them in real life. What jobs may use these skills? Create documents or posters that show this (e.g., Fractions Help Us When... posters).
- Teach students how to respond to different types of questions by drawing their attention to the language used and what each question is looking for. Again, a document camera can help you highlight key words for the class. Unpack the language so that students can decode what you are looking for on tests.

Physical Education

- Always begin with a review of the rules. Teach proper use of equipment and how to clean up. Get students thinking about why the rules exist by asking them what the rules should be and why different rules are good to have! Ask them to consider how the custodian would feel if the equipment was left scattered about, or how the principal would feel if they walked in and heard students making supportive comments.
- Perspective-take what they need to be successful with each activity. Students with autism do best in physical education when they have time to practice specific movements and skills before needing to integrate them. Teach step by step and model the actions required.
- You may need to teach specifics about personal space in games that involve tagging or throwing a ball to someone. Talk about the appropriate amount of pressure used to tag someone, where it is acceptable to tag someone, etc. Show it and then have students practice in an activity. Like my student Colin, who played tag using his keys, kids with autism may need help to understand how someone else experiences the same interactions. Clarifying these expectations from the beginning can prevent issues from arising.
- Some kids with (and without) autism have a hard time when feeling like they've lost a game. Initially, play low-stakes games where there isn't any winning or losing and that let students develop specific skills. Build up to competitive activities. Talk about and develop lists of what it means to be a team player, and how one person's goal is a point for the whole team, just like an assist is part of that goal. Encourage supportive comments (and talk quietly to students with autism to point out which comments might not be so helpful, and what to say or do differently next time).
- Gym can be overwhelming for students who may struggle with the sound, the motor skills required, and low self-esteem if they cannot easily pick up things the way their classmates do. It's important to create opportunities for participation and to get them to see why they're an important part of the group. Outline specific expectations for reluctant participants. Maybe they can take a break if they participate for one round. Maybe they need to watch a round or two first to see how it's done. If you can see they just want to be one with the bench, can you negotiate them being scorekeeper or setting up the equipment? Once you have discovered a job that resonates with them, speak to them before the next gym period and ask them to participate first with peers in the activity for a set amount of time before they take on this preferred role. Gradually increase your expectations for participation.
- Consider building in cool-down time at the end of the period so students can disengage from a group activity and do something on their own (e.g., stretching, playing with a ball). This can help them transition from activities that

> My colleague Sonia breaks down each skill long before we play a full game of basketball. She spends time practicing dribbling with both hands (so students can assess which is more comfortable), dribbling around pylons, dribbling around people, passing for short distances, passing from further away, passing to a partner who takes the shot (so students can practice what it feels like not to score but to contribute to the team), and much more.

demanded a lot of processing of information, social nuance, and physical coordination.

Social Situations

Consider situations from an autism lens. How does your specific student feel about a situation, and why? Remember, you may have two students with autism who both hate the recess bell, but it might be for two different reasons. One may hate the sound and one may hate having to stop what he or she is doing.

- If you aren't sure, ask! Listen to their perspective. My students surprise me all the time with what they're thinking, which is a reminder not to jump to conclusions about them.
- When you see it their way, you can help figure out what and how to teach them. If they get into a disagreement with a peer, you can have them identify other ways to handle the situation.
- Draw their attention to thoughts and feelings of others. Get them thinking about what others are interested in, what they like to talk about, and what they don't enjoy so much.
- Talk about your own thoughts and feelings, and how you handle those thoughts and feelings.
- Help them cope when things don't seem fair. Explain the logic—and roleplay, draw a comic, or make a chart. Visuals make a big difference!
- Students with autism don't always see why it's important to do what the group is doing or what an adult is asking. Explain why. Phrase requests in a way that shows the student is having a positive impact on you and the class (e.g., "Can you help me by turning out the lights?"). Notice when they are being a part of things and thank them for contributing.
- Enjoy their insights and ideas. They will be more willing to listen to you in the future if they feel appreciated and respected by you!

Tickets Out the Door

If Today Was a Video Game

This is a part I'd love to replay (I'd enjoy doing again):

I levelled up on (worked hard on/got better at)…

Something I'd change if it was in my control:

Player: _____

3 Things that STUCK with Me Today
(which means 3 Things I Found Memorable)

Name: _____

Pembroke Publishers ©2020 *The Autism Lens* by Kara Dymond ISBN 978-1-55138-347-7

3

Connecting the Dots

> **They Really Don't Know**
>
> Jeffrey is crushing Adnan on Rainbow Roads, the hardest lap of Mario Kart. Even I can see that. Jeffrey alternates between gloating and trash talking.
>
> "The most epic fail! You are seriously the worst player I've ever seen. My sister could beat you!"
>
> I sense a remote about to be thrown. So I put on the lens, the one that reminds me that my expectations do not always match what my students know to do. I beckon Jeffrey over and lower my voice. "I'm hearing you say comments that are likely to upset Adnan," I tell him. "Words like 'epic fail' and 'worst player ever'. Even if that were true, you shouldn't say it. We don't have to say every thought we think. Some thoughts we keep in our heads—especially if they will hurt someone else's feelings."
>
> I'm met with a blank look and then a dawning of realization. "Really!? Why has no one ever told me that before?"
>
> Twelve years old, and unaware that thoughts can (and should) be filtered. Imagine how much trouble you'd get into if you'd never learned this lesson! This is where the invisible disability comes into play. It is difficult to know what our students don't know. Jeffrey, like many of my students, was unable to view how his words or actions were perceived by others and often mistook his own experiences and opinions as objective facts. Somewhere along the way, he had internalized the rule to "always tell the truth" and applied it, liberally and without exception.

In my classroom, where the focus is on developing social awareness and related skills, students can earn time to play together on the Wii. Although this might seem like a reward, it is an opportunity for me to see where students are on certain skills, information I might not otherwise be privy to. I can't tell you how many students want to shut off a game the minute they're losing. They do this at home, when playing alone, but it is not socially acceptable when playing with someone else. The "reward" of time on the Wii helps me gauge what students may need to work on to have a successful hang-out session at a friend's house.

The moment with Jeffrey was a time I was glad I put on my autism lens and took the time to explain what I was seeing. I could have easily used a sharp tone and chastised him—this is probably a common experience for him. The problem with repeated admonishments is that they don't help us figure out what's really going on so we know what to teach, and they don't help the child to know how to interact differently. As the psychologist Ross Greene says, "Kids do well if they can" (Greene, 2008, p. 11). The grand irony of autism is that, while there's a brain-based reason why my students have difficulty perspective-taking, their actions are often misinterpreted by those around them, whose brains are more easily able to consider other viewpoints. We spend a lot of time focusing on changing the child, but we need to also hold the lens up to ourselves. Are our expectations clear and reasonable? Have we explained them all, or have we assumed our students should already know them? Is our classroom environment sensory-friendly? We can teach so much more once we begin to look for the invisible, but very real, barriers to meaningful learning.

In a wildly unpredictable world, we, as humans, cope by trying to control what we can. Our brains want to make sense of the chaos and mystery of why things happen when and how they do. For kids with autism, this is especially true. They cling to what they know to be reliable, like routines and schedules, and are reassured by order and rules that provide structure to help them navigate the world. Research has shown that people with autism are excellent at analyzing variables in order to figure out rules that govern how things work and what causes what, something called systemizing (Baron-Cohen et al., 2003). This research studied gender differences in systemizing and empathizing. When compared to neurotypical females, neurotypical males scored higher at systemizing and lower at empathizing. The autism group, made up of both females and males, demonstrated a more exaggerated form of the neurotypical male results. They scored dramatically higher at systemizing and lower at empathizing. This makes sense, because their brain wiring makes it easy to create a logical rule, but much more difficult to figure out someone else's emotions. In other words, while systemizing works for establishing certain reliable rules like "gravity means things fall down toward the earth," the downside is that you can't use systemizing to figure out people. People are not governed by "if x happens, they respond with y."

Another issue for people with autism is that rule-bound thinking is often not subject to change. Once a child with autism thinks they've learned something, it can be absolute in their minds. Take my former student, Ryan. He is now nearing the end of high school, and his mother and I catch up periodically about how he's doing. Once, while we were wrapping things up, his mother got a flurry of texts. She shook her head, exasperated, then shared, "Here's a perfect example of rigid thinking for you. Ryan won't open the front door for his brother! He's locked out of the house." For years, Ryan had exasperated the whole family by banging on the shared bathroom door in the mornings, rather than patiently waiting his turn. They eventually told him that they wouldn't open and would take longer in there if he interrupted. The behavior decreased and they thought that was that. Fast forward to this night in question. After dinner, his older brother arrived home without his house key. Naturally, he banged on the door, knowing Ryan was home. Through the mail slot, Ryan called out: "I'm not opening up! Don't you know banging is rude?" All those years ago, Ryan had learned the rule about not banging on the door, but never learned how the rule might need to change with the situation.

Clearly, this is problematic because there are exceptions to almost every rule. Rules cannot teach anyone how to respond to every possible situation in life. When we cling to rules that do not change with the variables, we become rigid. We see this all the time in children with autism. As part of their rule-bound thinking, their default is to do, say, or think what's familiar, even when it doesn't make much sense to neurotypicals. Often, autistic students are the only ones on the first warm day of spring wearing their winter coats, not realizing that parents sent the warm clothing just in case. While everyone else is running around without a coat on, they're decked out in mitts, hats, snow pants—the works! They often don't take the weather into consideration.

Doctors look for inflexible behaviors and an insistence on routines as one of the diagnostic criteria of autism (APA, 2013). We play into this a lot when dealing with kids with autism, using things like the "first, then" principle (Barton, 2013) where we ask them to do something less preferable before getting to do something more preferable, such as needing to do math before they doodle on a sketch pad, or setting a timer so that they have to transition once the buzzer goes off. These strategies can be effective sometimes, but we also must be sure we are teaching for flexibility. We don't want a student getting upset if it's 10:03 and the teacher hasn't started math yet.

Instead, we should teach students that some rules in life are more like rough guidelines. Some rules change any time we're with a different person; for example, students greet their principal differently than their Grandma or the cool kid in class. Many rules change with age. The trickiest part is that no one explains all of these rules to us. We're expected to watch and learn. This puts kids with autism at a big disadvantage, because they don't know what to watch for in the first place.

The Hidden Curriculum

Unstated rules are called *the hidden curriculum* (Smith Myles & Simpson, 2001) or *hidden expectations or rules* (Garcia Winner, 2017) and are comprised of the many social expectations that we expect people to know without having to be told. Everything we do is imbued with these hidden rules. Even something seemingly easy, like greeting someone, is an intricate task (Smith Myles & Simpson, 2001), requiring a person to know what type of greeting to use, what words to say, what tone to use, what body language is appropriate, whether to touch or not touch, how long to sustain eye contact or a handshake, and how to disengage! There is never just one rule that can be applied equally in every situation. The rules change based on who we're interacting with, how old we and they are, the setting, and many other factors. Some examples:

- How firmly to shake someone's hand
- How long to maintain eye contact
- How to tell when a question is hypothetical
- How to walk up to a group and join their conversation
- We do not comment on how smelly the washroom is at work
- Why it's expected to throw a tantrum as a small child but not as an adult
- Why you should use tongs and not your hands at a buffet

- Why we don't eat all the popcorn when sharing a bowl with friends
- Why it's okay for people to get in your personal space on a crowded bus but not during a casual conversation

For those people who don't learn through osmosis, hidden rules require conversations and explanations. I'm a big fan of Michelle Garcia Winner's work and the Social Thinking™ concepts she developed after several decades of work as a speech language pathologist. She frames behaviors in terms of *expected* or *unexpected*, rather than appropriate or inappropriate. This language removes the value judgment and gets students thinking about what others are thinking, what is expected in the setting, and why others seem to expect it. It promotes perspective-taking and social understanding, and helps any student who might be weak in the social domain but who has the cognitive strength to approach new situations with a framework that helps them to predict what these hidden rules might be, enabling them to understand how their behavior may be interpreted by others.

Using this approach in my day-to-day teaching, I will often show students a variety of pictures of people and have them articulate whether the behavior is expected or unexpected in the situation portrayed and whether the person would make a good impression. Some photos are fairly obvious, such as a friendly-looking person in a business suit. I like to hear their thinking, because often pictures can be interpreted more than one way.

Students also need tips to understand that what is expected in Grade 1 may be unexpected in Grade 7. For instance, many of my teenage students get upset and tattle when their peers swear at recess. This was how swearing was handled in the primary grades, and they probably received positive reinforcement for bringing it to a teacher's attention. In Grade 7, not only do peers react with antagonism to this kind of tattling, but teachers may not appreciate it. Increasingly through the junior and intermediate grades, students are expected to solve their own problems, and swearing at recess is not perceived as a big deal. If one of my students is struggling with this, I will explain to them that they will hear swearing in the school yard. Older students experiment with bad language because they see it as mature behavior (ironically, adults tend to swear less). If older students are swearing in the expected way, they follow the hidden rules, like not swearing in front of an adult. They may sometimes swear at a friend in a joking tone. Targeted swearing—with the intention of hurting a person and that happens repeatedly—could count as bullying, and so is unexpected and can be privately reported to a teacher. Oh, it's so hard to gauge for our kids who don't pick up on all the social cues!

It's also hard for us, as adults, to predict what they don't know. One summer, Danny started a new social group for adults with autism. One of the events they were planning to do was laser tag. Having never played laser tag, Danny was understandably nervous. I thought I did a good job of preparing him. I thought I'd covered all the bases. I'm an autism consultant, after all. I used my best strategies. I offered to go with him, and he gratefully accepted. We role-played how to pay, I showed him the website, I talked through as many of the hidden rules as I could think of. We talked about the pack he'd be expected to wear, which would vibrate and light up if he were hit by another player. We talked about the layout of the facilities. The day came, and as we were driving there, I looked over to Danny in the passenger seat. He was chewing his lip and his eyes were like those of a man being dragged to the gallows.

Garcia Winner uses her Social Thinking Methodology™ with students with autism, ADHD, non-verbal learning disabilities, and other needs, and has developed many useful classroom tools, books, and curricula.

In my class, I've shown a picture of a man in front of a garage in a sports jersey covered in mud. Students will sometimes say that it makes a bad impression because his appearance is so messy. When I reframe it by asking, "What if I told you he just played in a championship rugby game?" those grass and mud stains become indicators of a player giving it his all. One time, I showed a photo of a bored student, blowing her chewing gum into a giant bubble in class. Five students voted that this was a bad impression. One exclaimed, "It's great! If I were in her class, I'd know who's most likely to have gum to share and who to hang around more often!"

The Hidden Curriculum 39

"Danny, what's wrong?"

"I don't want to get shot!"

I'd forgotten to tell him they weren't real lasers! Defaulting to humor, I told him I'd never have offered to come with him if there was a chance I'd be shot. After reassuring him about the lasers, I pointed out that any organization using real lasers would be sued and shut down before you could say "lawsuit"! While Danny saw the logic of my words, his anxiety was still at peak. So, we made a deal: he would try it for 10 minutes. If he hated it, he could head to the exit point and we'd leave, no questions asked. Fortunately, Danny loved it and has gone back several times.

In retrospect, I wish I'd asked him how he was feeling earlier. I wish I'd asked him if he had any questions about this new experience. Maybe I didn't give him the space to voice his worry. I wish I'd considered that what's obvious to me isn't always obvious to him.

I tell this story to remind you: you won't always get it right. You will forget to mention something, some time. Forgive yourself when it happens. It happens to all of us. So we apologize for missing steps. And we learn from it. We let it strengthen our autism lens, so we can think through more clearly from our student's perspective, for next time. Remember: for all the times we get it wrong, there are many more times we get it right!

Student Story: Hidden Rules

In Grade 9 science I was getting a poor grade on these labs we were doing and didn't understand why (even after initially speaking to the teacher). On my next lab I received a poor grade. I decided to speak to my teacher again to ask her what I was doing wrong because I didn't want another poor grade on my lab. However, I learned that my approach was not the most effective. I had gone to ask my teacher while she was teaching a class. According to her, I was demanding an answer right then and there and she had to explain to me that she had no issue going over my lab but that she was currently in the middle of a lesson with another class and that I would have to come back at another time. I learned that I cannot expect people to drop everything they are doing to answer my questions. I didn't realize that I was doing anything wrong, I just wanted an answer. I have learned to try and be more patient as it comes across that I am being self-centred.

— Grade 10 student

Generalizing Skills and Situations

It's time to think about how most of us learn. When my two older siblings were young kids, my sister Krista convinced my brother Nick to insert a stick into a log. Like many early learners, they were curious about what was inside. Unfortunately, Nick's swordplay woke a bee's nest and he faced the brunt of an angry swarm, while my sister had enough time and distance to get away unscathed. To this day, Krista is afraid of bees. Although she might kill me for writing this, it's a perfect example of neurotypical learning. We can learn vicariously, are able to discern what to do or not do simply from evaluating how successful someone else is (Barkley, 2012), just as Krista was able to learn a valuable lesson from watching the experience of someone else. Most of us shape our understanding of

Social Confusion: autistic children can experience anxiety and self-doubt when navigating what to say or do in unfamiliar social situations.

the world from experiences—our own or those of others, good or bad. From this, we unconsciously absorb universal truths that we can apply in the future, like *don't poke a bee's nest.* This is called generalizing.

This is not how kids with autism learn most easily. They often don't pick up rules from watching what happens to others. They may continue to ask a question after a teacher has indicated to another student that it's not the right time. After having a negative experience, they may not instinctively try something a different way. They might not have the cognitive problem-solving ability or flexibility to think of alternative responses, and so may repeat the same social faux pas over and over (Attwood, 2007). I've seen autistic students who repeatedly try to engage with their peers by grabbing their snacks or continually telling a girl that they want to marry her, even when peers immediately recoil and tell them to stop.

People with autism have trouble generalizing—internalizing a rule they have gleaned from prior experiences that they can later apply to future similar situations (Tsang, 2018), like Krista did with the bees. I suspect they aren't processing events around them as learning experiences, so they aren't making the connections others rely on to see what is similar between past and present situations. This has implications for all types of learning. How often as teachers do we prompt students that "it's the same thing we did yesterday" when, in reality, all the variables are different? Kids with autism might struggle with this on a literal level, but also have trouble because they tend to focus on the details rather than the main idea of a task or concept (due to weak central coherence, which we'll learn more about in Chapter 5). They might need you to review the task because it seems brand new when some parts have changed.

Let's say you help students with autism self-advocate with peers who are teasing them. You give them words to say like, "Leave me alone" and tell them they can ask for help if that doesn't work. There are two possible things that could happen: 1) they might not see that the same problem-solving skills are applicable next time they are being teased because it's a different conflict, so they won't say "Leave me alone" or ask for help; or 2) they might memorize this as a steadfast rule and apply the same strategy in every disagreement, even when it's not helpful. Say they want to play a board game with a friend; the friend wants to play Connect 4 and they want to play Guess Who. They bicker for a moment, when the student with autism remembers what he or she must do in a conflict. "Leave me alone!" they say, effectively ending the interaction. They are, indeed, left alone—even though that wasn't at all what they wanted. Why might this happen? We use context all the time and in all situations, whether determining what a word means, what someone is feeling, what to look at, what to do, or what to say. However, people with autism have *context blindness* (Vermeulen, 2012): they are unable to use contextual information spontaneously and unconsciously to give things meaning.

In October 2018, I had the pleasure of hearing Dr. Peter Vermeulen give a keynote address on autism and predictive thinking (Vermeulen, 2018). He theorized that people with autism process their experiences of the world very differently from the way people without autism do. When a neurotypical person walks into a living room, they don't need to process all the sensory information because their brain can predict what the room will be like. The neurotypical brain needs to process only the information that is different from what they expect to perceive. This means the brain takes mental shortcuts all the time, by comparing what the person predicts they will see based on information they have stored—for

My student David once told me he was so anxious to get home each day so he could run around and make sure everything—furniture, objects, rooms—was where it was supposed to be. He wasn't aware that most of these details (and certainly the room layouts) were not going to change. He had to process this information consciously each time he entered the house.

instance, about a familiar object, place, event, or concept—against what they are perceiving. The brain is very good at generalizing information into schema, or a mental file folder of attributes related to many different topics. So their schema of their own living room is basically a mental image of what that living room usually looks like. They would also have more "general idea" types of schema, like what a typical living room might look like in someone else's house. Think right now about an acquaintance whose home you have never visited. Imagine them in their living room. You just relied upon a generic living room schema! Similarly, when walking into a grocery store, neurotypicals can rely on a generalized script of what behaviors, sights, and sounds are expected in a grocery store. On a more micro level, their minds also have schema of objects, like chairs, that helps them to recognize that, even with a week's worth of clothes obscuring most of it, a chair is still a chair. The neurotypical brain creates these categories effortlessly, and neurotypical schema are somewhat inexact and able to change (Vermeulen, 2012). Because neurotypicals can instantly reference these schemas, they now need to process only sensory information that is new or different from their predicted schema. This processing happens so instantly—in less than 200 milliseconds—that they are not even aware of processing anything (Vermeulen, 2012). Because they know what to expect in their living room (or the grocery store or the chair covered in laundry), they can remain calm and collected in most situations.

In contrast, people with autism don't start processing sensory information from a generalized schema. Instead, they process all the details and might miss the main idea of a situation (Vermeulen, 2012). If you can't see context, it's harder to generalize schema of what's appropriate in different places, in different situations, and with different people. This means students with autism don't have a guide or reference point for most concepts or situations.

There's some research that people with autism may be better at spotting differences than similarities (Happé & Frith, 2006; O'Riordan et al., 2001). Not only can it be distressing to them when things are out of place or not what they expected, but also they are more likely to notice these small changes. Similarly, an eye for difference may be why it's so difficult to generalize. They may be unable to unconsciously see what is transferable or relevant to a similar concept or situation and, therefore, likely to occur again. Autistic brains are always working in overdrive, cognitively processing information rather than subconsciously absorbing it (Attwood, 2007; Tsang, 2018; Vermeulen, 2012). Except in familiar situations where they have been taught an exact routine, people with autism usually have great difficulty creating schema or scripts that are flexible and able to adapt to changes in context. It makes sense they need more processing time and struggle with social problem-solving!

Dr. Temple Grandin is a professor, inventor, author, and public speaker with autism who has written extensively about autistic people, their learning, and how their minds lack the instant ability to categorize new information into concepts that non-autistic people rely on in everyday learning, socializing, and decision-making. She relates a story about having difficulty telling the difference between cats and dogs. She looked at pictures of both animals, cognitively processing their features, and trying to apply a schema or general rule. At first, she thought dogs were big and cats were small. Then she saw a small dachshund. It took her an enormous amount of conscious effort to process why other people categorized these animals the way we do—and she eventually concluded that cats and dogs have vastly different nose shapes (Grandin, 2007). Whether people with autism can't spot differences or can't spot similarities, the end result is the same. They have difficulty categorizing intuitively. They can create schema or rules, but with little flexibility and only with conscious effort.

This makes it hard to use context to guide behavior, because they don't notice the context. Case in point: I visited a student in his Grade 4 classroom right before the December break. His teacher warmly dismissed the class by saying, "Happy holidays, everyone!" Covering his ears, my student turned to me and insisted, "See? I told you she's mean!" I prompted him to consider what her face and body were doing (smiling, relaxed), and what the intention might be. We talked about how, in my classroom with only six students at a time, I can speak in a quieter tone, but if I had 30 students in my class, I'd have to speak loudly so everyone could hear. Only then was he able to stop and realize he had jumped to the wrong conclusion. He had attended to one detail (loudness) rather than the whole picture. Loudness does not always equal mean! This illustrates that, when children with autism do generate a schema, it is often very rigid and they do not account for evidence to the contrary without support.

Vermeulen (2012) reminds us that people on the spectrum improve at categorizing and learning general rules with age. They may never spontaneously process context, but we can help them to develop stronger schema by explicitly pointing out context cues and helping them to account for them. When we teach skills, we can be extremely specific about when, where, and how to use them, and when not, where not, and how not to use them, too. If we teach them the exceptions (like Danny's lasers that aren't real), it's less for them to figure out on their own later. We reduce the enormous stress it takes to process all the details.

We are always reading the room of life but, most of the time, our brains do this in the background for us. Thank goodness! Imagine, for a moment, that you are about to start a new job, or go to a party with people you don't know, or move to a new neighborhood you've never explored before. Those are the times we must put in a conscious effort to process information. If you aren't on full alert, you won't remember whose face matches which name. It's how we learn what each context requires of us so we can fit in seamlessly, assess whether these are Scrabble people or Cards Against Humanity people, and discern which paths are safer and more enjoyable to walk. What if you always had to be on alert like that? It would be exhausting! You'd be wracked with anxiety all the time. When I relate this way, it helps me understand my students much better.

Cognitive Learning Style

> Dwayne used to become extremely agitated when his peers joked around. He felt like an outsider and, despite his incredibly quick mind for academics, he couldn't keep up with the social nuances of Grade 5. "Ms. Dymond," he said, "I wish I lived in the Dark Ages when people had no senses of humor."
>
> "Dwayne, I hate to break it to you, but people still used humor, even then."
>
> "Then why is it called the Dark Ages? Wasn't everyone miserable?"
>
> "Humans have always joked around and made their own fun—especially when things were miserable! It helps people to cope."
>
> "IS THERE NO LOGIC?"
>
> "I hate to break it to you..."

For my in-services, I pull up news headlines like *MAN ACCUSED OF TOSSING GATOR INTO WENDY'S DRIVE-THRU WINDOW* (Moye, 2016) and *2 ARRESTED AFTER FIGHT OVER CRABS LEGS TURNS VIOLENT, POLICE SAY* (Fox News, 2016). When you first read these headlines, you are probably baffled. Why in the world would anyone do that? So ask yourself what you would need to understand these situations. More information. Context. Insight into the thoughts and feelings of the people involved. That original sense of bafflement is probably rare for you. Our autistic students are likely feeling this many times per day, in most of their interactions.

Children with autism crave logic. They want to understand how and why things are the way they are. Most autistic individuals can systemize very well, explaining the world around them by recognizing the constant rules that govern our lives (Baron-Cohen et al., 2003). While this suggests they can, in fact, generalize and categorize to some extent, the rules and categories they perceive may be very narrow and not subject to change, reducing their ability to connect a concept to their experiences and new knowledge (Plaisted, 2001). Unfortunately, a simple rule-bound approach works well only when things are predictable, and most things in life are not (Vermeulen, 2012). Autistic students haven't wrapped their heads around (not literally) the fact that there isn't always order or sense to things. Learning is difficult because of this, but also because, instead of generalizing subconsciously based on experiences, they learn best by cognitively processing concepts or expectations, which takes considerable effort. They need to see the logic. "Because I said so," is the most frustrating response an adult can give, because children with autism are usually seeking a genuine answer about why something is the way it is. They benefit from clear, direct instruction, without ambiguous language or humor that is hard to understand and demands even more processing time!

A dear colleague of mine helped me come up with an activity, using an old violin, to promote understanding about how students with autism learn. With parental permission, I go into my students' classes and teach about the strengths and needs of a specific student, how they learn, and how peers can help them. First, I ask for a volunteer who has never played a string instrument before. I give them the violin and the bow, and before they can lift a muscle, I ask the class to make a prediction: "How will it go?" *Terrible!* the class usually responds, with eager anticipation. Little do they know, the violin hasn't been taken care of. Strings are slightly loose and the bow hasn't been waxed, which I'm told is important, so no sound is produced at all. Typically, everyone laughs at the first attempt. I'll say, "Wait a minute, let me show you first!" and pull out my cell phone to display a video of a talented violinist. "Now, try again!" Still the brave volunteer can't do it. Finally, I ask the class what would help the volunteer to be able to play. *To be told exactly what to do, step by step.* Just like anyone trying to learn a new instrument, people with autism best absorb new information when they are directly told what to do and why, and have the chance to practice, practice, practice. This applies to all kinds of learning—giving a presentation, starting a conversation, participating in group work, asking someone to play at recess, problem-solving how to ask for something they need, preparing for a field trip. I'm sure you can think of many more examples!

The gift for pointing out flaws in logic can make autistic folks wonderful comedians in their own right. I suspect many observational comedians are on the autism spectrum: Jerry Seinfeld has made comments in the past about possibly having autism, while Hannah Gadsby and Michael McCreary have confirmed diagnoses.

The logical thinking style of an autistic person is an asset in many situations, as they see alternative solutions and question rules that don't make sense. Many have strong visual search skills, and so can spot patterns, mistakes, or changes between photos with ease (Happé & Frith, 2006; Vermeulen, 2012). They are perhaps better courtroom witnesses, as they may have fewer false memories (Beversdorf et al., 2000) and can make decisions without being swayed by emotional cues (De Martino et al., 2008). They can find more efficient ways of doing things, even if it goes against the norm, like when Jeffrey had the brilliant if unconventional idea to sleep in his school uniform to save time in the morning. They observe and ponder and point out the weird things neurotypical folks tend to accept without question; like, why do we say we value honesty, but only to a certain point? Why do we tell kids not to talk to strangers or, worse, accept gifts from strangers, and then have one day a year when children go door-to-door accepting candy from a whole bunch of people they don't know, and another day each year when some children receive presents from a mysterious breaking-and-entering old man? Thanks to my students, I've found myself questioning everything I do in the classroom and making sure I have an exceptionally good reason for it! If I don't, they help me to laugh at myself or how the neurotypical world runs.

Strategies to Help Connect the Dots

As teachers, we want to help our students understand their peers, our classroom expectations, the work we expect them to do, and the many interactions going on throughout the day. There's no one answer or strategy that works every time, which means we must be creative problem-solvers. We try something, evaluate its success, and adjust as needed. For our students with autism, we can start by making ourselves, our classroom environment, and our expectations predictable. Here are some ideas:

Listen to Understand

- Monitor student understanding so you know what to teach.
- Welcome their questions.
- Conference with them each week to discuss concerns and interests, and to build relationship.

Communicate Clearly and Directly

- Teach routines.
- Set times for organization, like tidying desks and organizing loose papers.
- Use direct instruction to teach what they are expected to do (e.g., for tasks, for tests, when problem-solving issues, when going on excursions).
- All students will benefit from having each task broken down, explained, and practiced, with the opportunity for feedback along the way.
- Use visual supports, such as pictures or exemplars, for the whole class; pair them with step-by-step instructions.
- Promote critical thinking by having students vote on what a Level 4 (A) work sample looks like compared to other levels.
- Think about what hidden rules are embedded in classroom tests, tasks, and activities. It might seem obvious, but explain it anyway. Teach these explicitly to level the playing field.
- If you forget a rule, revise and let them know; it's a learning opportunity for you both!
- Take time to explain why things are a certain way and how different people may see the situation differently.
- Teach for flexibility. Talk about the specific context the rules apply to, and how it might be different in another context.
- Out-logic them! Ask them to think about and try to articulate why something is important, or whether a previous approach worked. Give them the reasons. Explain to them why sometimes trying a different approach can yield a better outcome. You don't need to have been on the debating team; you just need to be able to articulate things clearly.
- Visuals—e.g., modelling, role play, diagrams, comic strips—can help them visualize what you want them to learn (and have the added bonus of letting

them map out the thoughts and feelings of others to build perspective-taking skills).

- Praise them with specific feedback, so they know what you're praising them for! Simply saying "Good job" can be confusing. Are you talking to them? What was it that was good about what they were doing? Remove the guesswork by saying instead, "I really liked how you raised your hand and waited to be called!"
- Redirect them with specific feedback about what you want them to be doing, such as "I'd like you to take out your science duotang, please." We do a lot of telling students what not to do, and autistic students do better when you tell them exactly what you want.
- If you want them to do it again tomorrow, remind them before it's expected (priming).

Prepare, Don't Scare

- Do your best to prepare them in advance for changes.
- Build in positive surprises so that they begin to associate change with good feelings.
- Pre-warn as time decreases, as they often lose sight of the time. Give time countdowns and tell them when to transition.
- Practice transitions before they are expected.
- Pick your battles! Avoid power struggles, punishments, or threats (see page 93 in Chapter 7 for alternatives).
- React in predictable ways so they feel comfortable approaching you.
- Give them processing time and space rather than expecting immediate compliance.

Adapt to Each Student

- Decide on one or two goals for your student with autism (and involve parents in reinforcing this goal in other settings). Be their coach and motivator around these goals. Explain the *why* and positively reinforce students as they work on these goals (see Chapter 7).
- Be creative in your approach. For instance, prepare a student who is reluctant to answer with a question in advance. For a student who blurts out in class, give them a notebook for thoughts they want to share later in case there isn't time for them to share during the lesson.
- Consider the long-term impact of behaviors. Children with autism might not observe how the rules change and so may continue to display behaviors their peers have outgrown, unless we teach them what's expected.
- Pay attention to the mood and anxiety level of students with autism, and reduce demands when they're nearing their limits.

Be Flexible

- Don't necessarily assign a time to everything. At times, try telling students "Snack is when math is over."
- 'Fess up to your own mistakes, to model how to handle these situations for the whole class.
- Negotiate deadlines or numbers of questions with students, when possible.
- Be someone you'd want to work for!

4

The Power of Personal Connection

> **Teaching for the Future**
>
> I learned the hard way that Eric did not like the Happy Birthday song. It was our first class back after the March Break and my first year as a teacher. Two students in the class had celebrated their birthdays so I warmly announced we would be singing to them. Panicked looks crossed their faces. "But Eric doesn't like the Happy Birthday song! We didn't even sing it at our parties because his parents called our parents…"
>
> Visions overwhelm me: of Eric at a restaurant when another table bursts out in song, wait staff streaming to the table with sparklers; Eric, all grown up, at an office when someone brings in a cake. I rationalize: on his birthday, absolutely, we can respect his wishes and celebrate how he likes. But does Eric really have the right to decide what happens on someone else's birthday?
>
> I want to point out that if I had ten students who all hated the Happy Birthday song, I'd probably handle this situation ten different ways. Some might have sensory sensitivities that make the song unbearable to listen to. Some might have experienced a terrible birthday event and are triggered by the song. Using all I knew about Eric, I made a call. It was the tensest singing of "Happy Birthday" in the song's history. Everyone looked nervous. Eric was kicking the couch in the corner and swearing. *Yikes*, I thought. *Did I make the right call?*
>
> Later, I called his mom to investigate. "We stopped singing it to him when he was three," she told me. "It really upsets him. He thinks it's for babies. We don't sing it at any of the family birthdays."
>
> "So Eric may not even realize this is a song he'll probably hear the rest of his life, in different places? I think it's important we work on this, so he's comfortable staying in the room when he hears it."
>
> Mom agreed with my somewhat wacky idea: in two weeks, on my birthday, I'd have students sing to me. We'd work with Eric to develop strategies to stay in the

Teaching for the Future   47

room, no singing expected. When I told Eric about it, he confirmed my suspicions. He was unaware he'd have to deal with the Happy Birthday song his entire life, and he had assumed people were being condescending when they wanted to sing it to children.

Now, I don't usually have students sing to me on my birthday. I also wouldn't try this strategy if I didn't have a great rapport with the student in question. Thankfully for us both, I did. The morning of my birthday, I received an anxious phone call from his mom. "It was an ordeal getting him on the bus!"

I reassured her, "We've got this under control!" (Hoping this was true.)

When Eric got off the bus, I let him know the time the class would sing. It wouldn't be a surprise. He'd get a reminder just before. He could ask for headphones if he wanted. I also let him know I had a good surprise for him. What trust it must have taken for Eric, so highly anxious, to believe me that the surprise would be something he'd like! I took him into the office to see a video of his favorite hockey player, Alexander Ovechkin, singing "Happy Birthday" to a young fan.

"Eric, do you want to watch it with the sound on or off?" I asked, after explaining what it was.

"Off!" he said, rocking back and forth on the spot.

So that's how we watched it, but we could make out all the words Ovechkin was singing. Eric was grinning from ear to ear.

"How do you think Ovechkin might be feeling during this?" I asked.

"Nervous." We talked about how we could tell. The context: a scrum of reporters, light bulbs flashing; the nonverbal cues: nervous smiles to his teammates.

"He didn't even know the girl. Why do you think he still bravely sang, in front of that crowd?"

"To make her feel special."

"Exactly. When we sing 'Happy Birthday', that's exactly what we want for our loved ones, or friends, or even acquaintances. We want them to feel good. No one actually LIKES the song—you're totally right, it's an annoying song. But we do it to show we care. And," I said and paused, evaluating the strength of our relationship, "you want me to feel special on my birthday, don't you?"

"Absolutely!"

"What do you think you could do to be brave—like Ovechkin!—when everyone is singing?"

"Think of hockey!"

"Awesome strategy. Give me five!"

And so it went to plan: I reminded Eric when it was almost time, so he could begin thinking of hockey. He smiled all the way through the song, and maybe even sang along a little bit.

It may seem like I invested a lot of work in this one incident but, in my job, I have to think long-term while also choosing my battles. Avoidance doesn't teach skills; it strengthens fears. What would Eric's reaction look like at 18? At 30? I also learned an important lesson: always investigate the *why* so that, before your student feels distressed by something, you can teach the skills they need to cope. Today, I am a more proactive teacher and would investigate how Eric was feeling before making any decisions about singing as a class. At that time, I pulled it off, not because I knew a ton about autism at the time, but because Eric and I responded well to each other, I had parent support, and I knew what Eric liked.

It has taken me the better part of a decade to realize the magic: relationships aren't just one-sided, existing simply for you to teach kids with autism to cope with the hard stuff and comply with your will. This bond helps you, too. Having that caring relationship encourages you both to keep trying when the going gets tough. It's what gets you to the other side. It's what teaches you the best lessons, and it's what keeps your heart in the job.

There are many qualities that help teachers support and program for all their students: creativity, knowledge of pedagogy, best practices, child development. But nothing is more important than the heart in your chest and how you use it to build rapport. Everything—*everything*—is easier when you have a positive relationship. Children, especially children with autism, know when you like them. Despite not being able to always pick up on deception from peers, they seem to have a sixth sense for whether adults genuinely care. Once they know that you do, once they trust you, everything else can fall into place. Children with autism are much less rigid when they feel comfortable with a person. They are more open to your feedback. You can work on the hard stuff together. (You can coach them to watch a surprise video on a day they're already on edge about surprises!) Because you make them feel safe, they are in a place where learning can happen.

Fostering Positive Rapport

Every year, I have a couple of students who are much more interested in adults than peers. They enter the classroom and want to hug me and my classroom partner Sonia, who is an exceptional Child and Youth Worker; they hang around us on breaks. On trips, they want to sit with us. They seem oblivious to their peers and will interact in mandatory board-game play or gym games because we expect it, not because they like it. If we'd let them, they'd wander out of the game and over to us. We must handle this delicately. At the beginning of our time together, these students usually like to talk our ears off about fish, a specific video game, geography, or whatever their thing is. As they learn more about showing interest in others, they begin to ask Sonia and me a billion questions about our interests, lives, and opinions. They come to really enjoy these interactions, and we can gently prompt them to join peers in conversations at the snack table. They'll grudgingly do it because they care what we think, because they like us, because they know we like them.

We brainstorm what to say and do with them. We coach. We give high-fives and say how proud we are of them for talking with peers. They glow from our praise. They begin to join classmates on their own, checking over their shoulders to see if we notice. We give a thumbs up from across the room. Eventually there comes a time when they stop checking for our approval. We see the enjoyment, once only experienced with us, experienced with peers.

It isn't always easy to build relationships, and with some students it may take half a year. Stick with it. Craig taught me that, while some kids may be easier to connect with, they all crave connection. And we, as their teachers, can often be the bridge between them and their peers.

Of course, I've also had students who are much more difficult to win over. One family practically dragged a new student, Craig, to visit our classroom and to meet us for the first time. We have private visits before the program starts so our new students can get a tour, play on the Wii, test out the bean bags, and hopefully not feel so anxious on the first day. Craig was not having any of it. He screamed for a good half hour, with his parents trying to calm him down. We stepped out of the room to give them space. I'm sure we handed them a book with photos of the classroom to help him with the future transition and tried to look reassuring, but all five of us were worried.

Our first-year group was an energetic, funny, special group of kids. Though Craig enjoyed their company, he certainly screamed a few times a day the first month or two and his body was always tightly wound, arms stiff with anxiety. He also screamed frequently at his home school, whenever something new was being introduced or when he felt he couldn't meet expectations. And of course, the students at his home school wanted little to do with him. How lonely he must have been. But in our program, the kids seemed to understand (with coaching from us) to give space and look away when he was upset and to invite him to play when he wasn't. We didn't respond with anger to his upset moments, and so they didn't last very long. He'd quiet down and ask for help or do what, initially, he had been too anxious to try. Eventually, Craig's desire to be with his buddies, talking and joking around, playing on the Wii (even if he lost), was motivating enough to help him overcome the anxiety of being in a group setting, and the screaming dwindled to a halt. During the first few months, he was invited to his first birthday party by one of our students, which was a first for several in our class!

It was the first day back after the winter break, when several students were hugging me goodbye for the day, that Craig spontaneously hugged me, too. He'd missed our lovely little class. He'd missed his peers, and I like to think he'd even missed me. It was hard earned, and a hug I will never forget. And his learning took off because he finally felt safe.

Ways of Fostering Rapport

- **Be present.** Turn your body to face them during interactions.
- **Smile lots!**
- **Physically get down to their level.** Sit or kneel by them. Towering over anyone can increase their anxiety. Be mindful of your body language.
- **Show interest in their interests.** Learn what you can about the topics. Ask them questions. Remember what they say!
- **Learn and tell jokes they'll like.** I know so many video game jokes now!
- **Play with them.** Play a game during an indoor recess. Play a game for a lesson. At the end of one school year, I let my students drench me in a water gun fight. We reviewed rules, of course, like don't hit anyone with a stream of water in the face, or when they do not have a working water gun. It was, literally and figuratively, a blast. They delighted in soaking me! Sonia was the adult and took pictures.
- **Capture the memorable moments in pictures.** Create a class photo board so there is always a visual reminder of the good times they've shared with you and peers, friendly interactions, successful moments, and other positive memories. Share photos with parents so they can see their child enjoying being a kid! (All with proper permissions, of course.)
- **Try out their favorite activities on your own time.** If you can, play video games they like, at least once, so you can talk about it with them.
- **Ask for their input.** My students love solving my computer problems or helping to set up the Wii. I ask them what I'm doing wrong and let them be experts. I also ask them to suggest songs to play for song of the day, as long as their choices can tie into what I'm teaching and are appropriate (I preview in advance). They love having a say in what happens in the classroom!
- **Ask them their opinions on classroom activities.** Remember what they like, and next time you pull out that board game say, "I picked this because I remembered you like it." There is nothing more meaningful to a child than being seen, heard, and remembered.
- **Begin each day with a clean slate.** Especially when a child is having difficulty self-regulating, we have to make them feel safe and valued. If possible, begin the day giving these children special jobs.
- **Invite their questions.** Use an anonymous question box for privacy or let them write questions for you in journals or Tickets Out the Door. This way, you have a sense of their concerns, worries, and learning interests.

Last year, my students wanted to mark the occasion of my birthday (although there are two birthday stories in this book, I swear, this isn't something I actively encourage!). When I was on my lunch break, they sat together and planned this card as a surprise to show they were thinking of me. One of the artists in the group drew everyone in the class and they all contributed to a message inside. It stayed on my desk until June and is now in my Happy Thoughts box! Whenever I look at it, it reminds me of the importance of creating a classroom where everyone feels they belong.

I begin each day with what I call a 4-Square sheet. The page is divided in four, and each quarter has a question or sentence starter. Students respond in pictures, words, or both. It often gives me insights into their interests, goals, worries, and much more. The 4-Square sheets help guide my instruction and follow-up during individual conferencing.

50 *The Power of Personal Connection*

> **A question I have about having conversations is . . .**
>
> How can you stay on topic?

> **A question I have about making friends is . . .**
>
> why we sometimes break up

> **A question I have about autism is . . .**
>
> Will my adult life be hard

- **Thank them, often.** I try to catch opportunities to thank students in the moment, and also take time at the end of each day to write down kind actions and successes that happened during the day. This has the added benefit of making you more aware of the good all your students do and the progress they are making; the more grateful we are, the happier we are.

- **Send sunshine emails** to parents describing lovely moments when you observed their child helping someone out, trying something difficult for them, or naturally and successfully interacting with their classmates. I guarantee their parents need to hear it!

- **Reward effort.** Consider spontaneous rewards that draw on your student's talents or interests like, "You got right to work, without any reminders. You've been working on that goal, and I'm so impressed. Why don't you take five minutes to make origami?" Rewards make behaviors much more likely to happen!

- **Let them know how much you enjoy having them in the class.** Highlight specific gifts they bring to the classroom in a note, in a private conversation, or in front of the class, depending on their comfort level with feedback. Find something to praise every day.

- **Use humor they can understand and enjoy.** I once was losing my voice and so taught part of the day using a text-to-voice app that made me sound like a robot. My students loved it and listened more attentively than ever before. While it caused me some dismay to realize I'm more interesting as Robo-Dymond, they thought it was hysterical and it remains a shared happy memory we reference from time to time.

- **Devote a portion of your wall to a classroom art gallery.** The art can rotate (as it does at all galleries) once it gets too full. My students take advantage of this display of their talents!

- **Really listen.** Ask follow-up questions. Especially because we want them to show more interest and attention to others, we need to model it. Then, once they like that feeling, we can prompt them. "You know, we've talked a lot about your interests. Can we talk about my cats? I really like when you show interest in the things I care about, too." Thank them for doing this, too.

Fostering Positive Rapport

Social Differences

What Art Class Feels Like For Me: autistic youth often feel a heightened sense of being scrutinized that adds to their anxiety.

Think for a moment about a time when you felt completely out of place. Maybe you didn't know anyone. Maybe you were in a different country. Maybe you weren't an expert on the topic in a room full of people who were. That feeling doesn't even come close to how our students with autism feel after years of not getting it right in most of their interactions. Conversations, games, group work, and even seemingly innocuous exchanges like greetings involve a myriad of social nuances and reciprocity that can be foreign to these children.

In his memoir about his experiences growing up without knowing he was autistic, John Elder Robison talks about making several attempts when he first started school to befriend a girl named Chuckie. First, he petted her like a dog, remembering advice his mother gave him about how to befriend animals (there's that rule-bound thinking without consideration of context). Then, when that didn't work, he got a stick and tried again, thinking how dogs liked sticks. It was not successful, with student or teacher! He regrouped the next day and tried to tell Chuckie how to play with the trucks in the sandpit. Chuckie was having none of it. The next time, he tried to impress her with all his dinosaur knowledge. She rebuffed this attempt. Humiliated, he never tried to socialize with his peers again (Elder Robison, 2007). His experience is not uncommon. I've had students articulate that they just don't know what they're doing wrong, but acutely feel that it's they who are, in fact, the ones messing up.

What might this look like? In conversations, they may run on and on, not picking up on the boredom of the listener, or they might be hard to follow because they don't understand the listener's perspective (Attwood, 2007; Lee et al., 2018). They may not know to filter their thoughts or words in a way that does not offend others, and so can be perceived as rude or uncaring (Attwood, 2007), like my student who didn't see "loser" as an offensive term because the student he applied it to had literally just lost a game. Yikes! They may not show listening skills when someone else is talking and may walk away before a teacher or peer is done speaking to them. Some students with autism have selective mutism, which means they are unable to speak in certain contexts. All these communication difficulties affect their ability to strengthen relationships with others.

As teachers, we tend to be more concerned about academic performance than recess skills, for obvious reasons: we are accountable for teaching and assessing, and we have limited hours in the day! However, social and self-regulatory skills of children are predictors of future success across all areas (Jones et al., 2015), and you know how children learn these skills? Through play. In fact, I think of play and group work as on a continuum. As young children play with others, they begin developing vital interpersonal skills they will need to interact with others for the rest of their lives. When bossiness doesn't get them far, they learn to persuade others to do things their way. When they hurt someone's feelings, even if they're right, they learn that apologies smooth things over and mend any hard feelings. They learn to cooperate, negotiate, compromise, agree to disagree, and express thoughts in a way that serves their interests—all skills that require theory of mind (see perspective-taking, page 25 in Chapter 2), weighing consequences, and thinking of long-term benefits versus the immediate short-term benefits of just grabbing the toy car they want to play with.

Kids with autism get far less practice at developing these skills than other children. Many don't have play opportunities outside of school. They may not be

52   *The Power of Personal Connection*

invited to birthdays or get-togethers. Many of my students' well-meaning family members got in the habit of letting them win or end games if they were extremely frustrated as toddlers or young children. Whatever the reasons, lack of play experiences for autistic children means they are not equipped to cope with loss or disappointment, and so may appear developmentally much younger when put in these types of situations later. They also might gravitate toward much younger children, who are more at their level in game play and more predictable, or they might seek out adults, who are generally more patient than same-age peers (Attwood, 2007). They have particular difficulty figuring out the rules to games and, once the rules are taught to them, have trouble coping if the rules change.

It's also worth mentioning that the school yard is a noisy, sensory-overload–inducing place. If you've ever tried to find a specific kid at recess at a large school, you have an inkling of what the environment might be like for a child with autism, who not only needs to identify who to join, but also how to join them before they can participate in games or hanging out. They aren't doing this in a quiet clinical environment with a therapist coaching, but in the real-time dynamics of the Lord-of-the-Flies recess yard. If they can find who they want to approach, they might not know what to do next. They might freeze or try initiating the wrong way. I've seen children with autism try jumping on the backs of peers or standing ten feet away from the person, not knowing how to get their attention. Once they're in a game, they can struggle with physical coordination or prediction of what will happen next (Sinha et al., 2014), making it exceptionally difficult for them to integrate in team sports.

They often cope with these intensely overwhelming and often painful social experiences by fixating on the rules or delving more deeply into their favorite subjects and interests (Attwood, 2007). It's easier and less stressful to retreat into their imaginations or solitary activities, which can be a much-needed break; it might also be a signal of their discomfort and confusion around joining or maintaining interactions. Some of my students have described studying others, trying to figure out how everything social seems so easy for others, but not for them. What on earth are the hidden rules?

During a unit on the Zones of Regulation (Kuypers, 2011), a budding artist in my class drew this scenario when prompted to show a time he felt a Blue zone emotion (sad, bored, tired, hurt). It reflected a sense of isolation he never voiced or reflected in outward behavior. We have to be ever vigilant not to let our quietest kids fall through the cracks!

Bullying

Children with autism are frequent targets of bullying. They can be targeted four times as often as their peers (Little, 2002). Forrest and colleagues (2019) found two reasons associated with greater risk of being victimized by bullies: not being

I also wonder whether the impulse to tattle and over-correct might be a reflection of how often these children are themselves over-corrected. While other kids can be kids, children with autism and other exceptionalities are under constant scrutiny for their errors.

socially tuned in and resistance to change. These children can be easily manipulated by peers posing as their friends. One of my students shared how he flooded a science classroom after classmates told him to pull the string on the emergency eyewash station. He didn't know what would happen, while his peers knew to make themselves scarce. He got in trouble and his peers did not.

Given their difficulties with theory of mind (predicting the thoughts, feelings, and intentions of others), autistic children make many social mistakes that set them apart from or bother peers (Attwood, 2007), and that includes peers who might otherwise be sympathetic. Children with autism may not see their impact on others and so do not adjust what they do or say to improve relationships. For instance, many students with autism can take abiding by rules to its limits, policing classmates' behaviors, like the time one of mine said, "Ms. Dymond, they were running in the hallway! Shouldn't they get in trouble?... Well I WAS chasing them, but they didn't have to run!" Peers, not understanding that this is the function of a neurological difference, are put off by tattling and over-correction. This is not, in any way, a justification of bullying, but rather an explanation: social isolation puts autistic children at greater risk of being targeted. Without a network, the protective factor of a social group (Cappadocia et al., 2012) does not exist.

Children with high-functioning autism are at greater risk of being bullied when compared to neurotypical peers and to peers with autism combined with an intellectual disability, and they are at the greatest risk if they also have anxiety or depression (Forrest et al., 2019; Hwang et al., 2018; Zablotsky et al., 2014). In a study of parent surveys, it was tallied that 94% of children with Asperger Syndrome or a nonverbal learning disability were targeted by bullies within the previous year (Little, 2002). They are targeted more often when integrated in inclusive classrooms, as compared to students with autism who are only partially or rarely integrated into general classrooms (Maïano et al., 2016; Sterzing et al., 2012; Zablotsky et al., 2014). Peers who know better than to pick on a classmate who can't help being different might not recognize the same is true of under-the-radar kids with autism, whose invisible disability is harder for peers and teachers to identify (Garcia Winner, 2013). Consequently, these students may be shunned by those peers who might otherwise be understanding or who could be allies against bullies.

Although included in the physical setting of the classroom, children and teens with autism report significant loneliness and less satisfying friendships than neurotypical peers (Bauminger & Kasari, 2000; Locke et al., 2010). Social problems for autistic students can worsen in adolescence, when these students experience more active exclusion from social structures (Locke et al., 2010), particularly as student cliques solidify. As the social dynamics become more complex in each consecutive grade, peers also become more subtle in their bullying; they recognize that physical abuse is likely to get them into trouble and increasingly use verbal or relational bullying like shunning, which is harder for adults to detect (Cappadocia et al., 2012).

Students with autism may also have difficulty in accurately identifying bullying, with some students ready to shrug off anything their peers do and others quick to jump to the conclusion that everything is bullying. In one study on the ability of autistic children and youth to gauge social appropriateness (Loveland et al., 2001), participants were shown two types of scenes: verbal and nonverbal scenes depicting inappropriate behaviors. The autistic group could usually identify the correct behaviors. And when comparing scenes without words to ones where the inappropriate behaviors were conversational gaffes, they found it

54   *The Power of Personal Connection*

easier to identify nonverbal infractions. But when asked to evaluate why a behavior was inappropriate, they struggled to give answers that made sense by using context or perspective of others. This goes to show that, despite their own command of language, they have great difficulty recognizing intentions or impact of others when processing language.

I've worked with many students who are hypersensitive and perceive peers as bullying them, even when it is unintentional or friendly teasing. Research shows that youths with autism can be likely to misinterpret non-bullying situations as bullying, especially if they have experienced frequent negative interactions in the past (Maïano et al., 2016; Van Roekel & Scholte, 2010). This may predispose them to see future situations as bullying, even when others around them do not. This brings to mind a student who would plug his ears whenever classmates asked him to stop doing things, whether it was to stop talking about his knowledge of world geography or to stop knocking over their snow castle at recess. Any negative feedback was perceived as bullying, which elicited a dramatic reaction from him, and everyone ended up frustrated. In situations where children with autism are being bullied, they may respond in a way which is either too passive to stop the bullying or so reactive that it makes a bully enjoy bothering them (Attwood, 2007).

> **Regardless of whether their experiences of bullying are real or perceived, autistic children are more likely to suffer from mood disorders, hyperactivity, self-injury, and oversensitivity (Cappadocia et al., 2012). As we all know, this can have a terrible impact on all aspects of a child's development.**

Studies show that kids with autism can also engage in bullying behaviors; however, this perpetration could, in fact, be unintentional. Teens with autism who were rated as bullies by teachers and peers typically had less-developed theory of mind and so misinterpreted bullying as non-bullying, unaware of their impact on others (Van Roekel & Scholte, 2010). In a large-scale study of bullying in over 22,000 children, Hwang and colleagues (2018) determined that autistic children were less likely to deliberately bully when compared to peers. They also attributed this to weak theory of mind (perspective-taking) and raised concerns that peers or teachers might misinterpret their actions as bullying because they are typically blunt and don't perceive their own impact on others. Some autistic students in the study had additional diagnoses that presented with aggression, which could also be perceived as bullying. It's worth mentioning that research by Crick and Dodge (1996) of aggression in children—not specific to autism—showed that these children think differently about aggression, either seeing aggression as a way to solve problems quickly or to achieve desired goals, or misreading peers' intentions as hostile and provocative. When I've taught students presenting with autism combined with aggression, I've observed distorted rule-bound thinking, such as, "In my culture, we hit to discipline, so this is okay," or "My parents said I should defend myself against bullies and that's why I can use my karate moves against someone who bugs me." While comments about self-defence or different cultural norms may have been made by families with the best of intentions, they probably were also highly context-specific. For rule-bound thinkers who are context-blind, that rule becomes *the* one rule to live by. When we see this rule-bound tendency in a child who misinterprets bullying or who does not understand there are other options for responding to teasing or bullying—like a snappy comeback, ignoring, walking away, seeking out friendly peers, and getting adult help—statements like this set them up for disaster. So while children with autism may appear to bully on occasion, they are much more likely to be victims of bullying (Maïano et al., 2016). Either way, they need our help.

Social Differences

Long-Term Outcomes

You've probably heard the comment, "Oh, but they're high-functioning. They'll be okay. You can't tell." That might be the problem. Individuals with "high-functioning" autism do not necessarily fare better in the long run than others on the spectrum when considering health, mental health, employment, relationships, and independence (Baldwin et al., 2014; Gal et al., 2015; Hillier et al., 2018; Howlin, 2003; Lounds Taylor, 2017; Southby & Robinson, 2018). Compared to all other disability groups, high-school graduates with autism have the lowest rate of employment and post-secondary education (Shattuck et al., 2012), which certainly seems to suggest they need to be connected to better supports. Unfortunately, they often do not qualify for autism services, because of age and perceived functioning level (Southby & Robinson, 2018).

I tell parents that nothing is off the table. People with autism and average to above-average cognitive abilities can be very capable of post-secondary education, marriage, employment, parenthood, and other milestones; however, only with the right preparation and supports. Autistic students at university report many invisible barriers, including inadequate supports or a lack of faculty or staff understanding (see review, Hiller et al., 2018). They feel particularly lost when dealing with emotions and executive function skills in their new environment, rating their quality of life as significantly lower than their peers (Dijkhuis et al., 2017).

> In the workplace, social skills can be the difference between being hired or promoted or not, and are often valued more than the ability to get the job done (see review, Baker-Ericzén et al., 2018). Ability to excel at the job could be undermined by an inability to effectively converse with a client or with workmates. Perhaps because of social communication difficulties and their invisible disability, adults with high-functioning autism tend to be overrepresented in part-time or unstable positions, are often overqualified, and report both social isolation and a lack of accommodations (Baldwin et al., 2014; Gal et al., 2015). Research shows they have worse employment rates than those with intellectual disabilities (Taylor and Seltzer, 2011, as cited in Baker-Ericzén et al., 2018).

If we consider the whole picture—a lifetime of feelings of being different and being on the outside, and often expectations to perform better than they can—it's unsurprising that health and mental health are ongoing concerns for people with autism. Autistic adults are significantly more likely to have a mood disorder or to consider or attempt suicide, and have poorer health in general (Croen et al., 2015; Vohra et al., 2017). By adulthood, as many as three-quarters of adults with autism can experience significant mental health concerns (Moss et al., 2015, as cited in Hickey et al., 2018). Suicide is the leading cause of premature death for individuals with high-functioning autism (Hirvikoski et al., 2016, as cited by Mandell, 2018), and attempts are made nine times more often than in the general population. Are there warning signs? Absolutely. Significant anxiety is experienced by roughly 40%, and clinical depression by 36%, of children with autism (Cai et al., 2018). Thoughts of suicide occur in 11% of autistic children, and roughly half make an attempt (Mayes et al., 2013b). Think about that for a moment. *This starts when they are in our care.* These are our kids. They are struggling. They are isolated. And they need our help.

The Social Gap

Although they might not be the easiest to spot, social differences can have a profound impact on students with autism, for whom the social gap widens with age. When we think about their recesses and social opportunities at school as compared with peers, it is clear that their peers get more better-quality practice with interpersonal skills, and so continue to develop on a steep upward trajectory while students with autism lag behind. Then suddenly we expect autistic students to participate in group work and have those skills that are rarely explicitly taught. My fear is, without our support, guidance, and influence on peers, kids with autism will continue falling through the cracks. How will this affect their

Why is independence always touted as the only end goal for autistic kids? We should emphasize interdependence equally. Support systems help us all to feel cared-for, to be better able to deal with big feelings, to know we're not alone when problem-solving, and to recognize we are no less valuable when asking for help than when helping others. Feeling a part of a community is vital to quality of life and positive mental health.

long-term relationships and employability? Most importantly, what is the impact on their emotional well-being?

It doesn't have to be this way.

One of the greatest joys of my job is that moment when my students begin recognizing fellow classmates as friends. After three years together, and an overnight trip to an outdoor education centre, one of my groups agreed that, "Now we're all even closer than family." When I think back to how socially isolated they all were only a few years before, it fills me with hope.

Teachers can make a transformative difference for these kids. The first step is recognizing that all children with autism need help socially. For some, the lack of skills will be obvious. Yet we often forget that quiet children with autism also need help; just because they may not be in the middle of arguments or having frequent meltdowns doesn't mean they're fine. Social isolation isn't always a preference, but can be a signal that a child is at a complete loss at what to do to be successful with peers. Considering how the bulk of their social opportunities will occur in school hours, we need to give them a chance to experience quality social practice.

We can create opportunities for interactions in the classroom and at recess. We can ensure our techniques for creating teams or groups does not leave out anyone. We can explicitly teach skills they may need when engaging in partner or group work. We can connect them to peer buddies. And maybe, just maybe, we might introduce them to their first friend.

Strategies for Unstructured Times

Group Work

Keeping in mind that children with autism need guidance to figure out the hidden rules, it helps to begin by structuring what interactions you can. Consider times students are at risk of being left out, like when forming groups, teams, or seating plans, and try to structure this for success. This is all part of differentiating the classroom, and will help your other students, too.

- **Be mindful to create groups in ways that don't further isolate kids with autism.** Try to form groups with understanding peers or someone they like. If you are letting students pick their own groups, you may wish to pick a group leader who chooses one peer to be in their group; you place the remaining students in the group. This way, no one suffers the humiliation of being picked last. I saw how well this worked in one of my students' classrooms and there was no grumbling. It was fair, everyone got a turn at some point to be a leader and pick a friend, and those tougher-to-place kids were not placed last. Make it part of the culture that everyone works with everyone.
- **Give them roles,** as in literature circles. This is clear-cut for autistic students, and gives you a chance to let them shine if they have a particular talent.
- **Before work periods begin, explicitly talk through hidden social rules that occur during group work.** What are their roles? How should they share ideas? How should they *not* share ideas? How should they pick or express opinions? What do they do if they disagree? Challenge your whole class to think about these social issues. It will prime all of them to use better interpersonal skills and work through the tricky parts of group work.
- **Teach the class to use friendly reminders,** using a calm tone of voice, to ask someone to do something a different way. If it doesn't work, they can come to you for help, but the goal is to have students try to work through disagreements on their own.
- **Circulate and coach as needed,** praising groups and students when you see supportive language and collaboration.

Strategies for Unstructured Times 57

- **Set up strategic partnerships.** You may wish to engage your more understanding students in coaching and looking out for students with autism or others who might be lost in a group.
- **Move from structured to less-structured.** While structure helps students with autism feel more comfortable and confident participating, it's also important to reduce structure at times to build flexibility and to assess how they handle a situation. My general procedure is to begin the year with high structure and gradually relax it. If you've been grouping students very deliberately since September, you could say, "You've been great group members and have learned how to work well with one another. Another important part of being in a group is learning to pick your own groups. How do we do that? What do we do if someone asks to join our group that isn't our favorite person?" Then coach group creation that doesn't leave out anyone or have students reacting negatively if they have to be in a group with someone they dislike.
- **Work toward independent problem-solving.** You may also challenge students to sort out their own roles. How do they divide work fairly? If Martha and Henry both want to write on the bulletin board, how do they solve this problem? Give them rules, such as *Everyone must agree to the plan of what to do and who does what before anyone begins writing things down*. You could structure non-structure by having them submit their signed plan before they get to begin!

Recess

- **Teach recess games during gym or DPA** to help establish rules that everyone knows, reducing some of the ambiguity that can prevent kids with autism from participating spontaneously.
- **Make a plan.** Before recess, talk to your autistic student(s) about who they might spend time with and what would be a good activity to do together. If they'd prefer to hang out and talk, brainstorm what might be good to talk about. Send them out with recess equipment they know how to use and encourage other students to ask to join them in a game.
- **Structure lunch recess**, which is typically twice as long as morning and afternoon recesses and can be exceedingly difficult for students with autism to manage. This would be a good time to arrange for them a job in the office or helping with younger students.
- **Consider offering a non-sport club** (e.g., Lego, art, mindfulness, board games) and encouraging your student to join or help out. Two of my students were thrilled not long ago when they proposed an Anime Club and a teacher agreed to supervise!
- **Check in after recess** and ask students with autism who they played or talked with and how it went. This can help you set different goals for them for next time. For instance, if they struggled to start a conversation, brainstorm a phrase to try out.
- **When you are on duty, keep an eye out for any student who tends to be alone.** Try to engage them and let their teachers know.

Maintaining an Inclusive Climate

- **Respond to rudeness, mean teasing, and bullying** so that students know unequivocally that you will not tolerate them, wherever you happen to encounter them.
- **Have a system in place for students to anonymously report** if they see someone being bullied or if they experience bullying themselves.
- **Problem-solve smaller conflicts affecting most of the class using a classroom community circle,** which allows everyone to express their perspective and work through to a solution.
- **When you design seating arrangements, try not to put all the kids with differences together, apart from everyone else.** Sometimes this is done so that those students can be closer to the front or so it's easier for support staff to help them all at the same time, but it can serve to isolate them. Find out from children with autism who they might like to sit with. While this could need to change throughout the year, be sensitive to seating dynamics.
- **Peer buddies** can be helpful, so long as they don't do everything for students with autism. Teach them how to give friendly reminders to classmates when they appear to need help.
- **Teach about differences** (without singling out a student or sharing their identification without permission). Prompt the class to think of ways they could include someone who had trouble joining games or conversations (e.g., they could invite, explain rules, greet, start conversations they know the other person would like, etc.) or who has trouble understanding their impact on others (e.g., "Not everyone realizes how they come across. How can you let them know in a way that won't make them think you're being rude?").
- **Reflect different ways of thinking and being in the literature you read** (see Resources on page 123). Make it okay to discuss strengths and weaknesses and to celebrate all the kinds of thinkers in the room. You could even poll the class about what their strengths are and represent the data on a bar graph, a class expertise chart, or some other organizational concept you are teaching.
- **Explain that everyone is working on different things, and you support students sometimes in different ways.** There are many great activities and visuals online that you can use to explain equity in the classroom.
- **Have an inclusion challenge for the whole school.** Each month make a different class responsible for coming up with a new inclusive practice to implement. This could be anything: a bulletin board where thank-you messages are written by teachers and students when someone else makes them feel good; a buddy bench where children know to go if they're alone and want someone to spend time with; intermediate students being peer recess coaches and organizing simple games (with some adult coaching, as needed); etc. Everyone is much more likely to get on board if they see their ideas in practice.

Strategies for Unstructured Times 59

Promoting Peer Relationships

- **Find out if your students with autism have friends.** If you don't know who they gravitate toward, ask! Social interaction is so important for all students' development that, if you have time, you could ask all parents at interviews whether their child has opportunities to connect outside of school with other kids. This will give you an idea about who else might need more support to help build relationships.
- **If they are more adult-oriented, engage students with autism in conversations about special interests** so that they learn they can enjoy time with others, and then include others in these conversations. Gradually expand their social circle.
- **Watch for misunderstandings.** One of the biggest barriers to peer relationships is misunderstandings between autistic students and their peers. When you can, watch how things are going at unstructured times. Sonia and I often watch from windows, where our undetected presence means kids don't change their behaviors.
- **Debrief them.** Get your students with autism to talk about encounters with others so you can monitor their understanding of social interactions and coach as needed, debriefing misunderstandings about peers or staff when they occur.
- **Talk to students with autism about a social goal for the week.** Ask them if they have any ideas. If not, suggest a goal that is just out of their comfort zone, but at their level. Maybe all you want is for them to physically move so their body is near a classmate's at lunch. Maybe you challenge them to ask peers about their interests, and give them a list of questions they might ask. If your classroom culture allows everyone to work on different things, you can ask peers to help by doing the same for your students who are learning these skills.
- **Use get-to-know-you activities.** September is a perfect time to work on All About Me activities and to compile responses into a class book. One of my students wasn't interested in talking to peers until he saw how many of them liked Minecraft; he took ten minutes every morning looking through the book and selecting a peer to talk to. The class knew he was working on conversation skills and were happy to help. The book also helped him to remember classmates' names.
- **For a whole-class approach, have a daily or weekly mix-and-mingle** where students are expected to have short conversations with a variety of peers on a topic you provide, moving on to another peer when the music changes. If this is too overwhelming for students, you could try a set-up more like speed dating: half the class remains seated and their partners rotate. Keeping the student with autism on the seated side reduces transitions and could help decrease anxiety. I'd limit it to a few exchanges and one or two rotations.
- **Drama games can help classmates appreciate what they have in common.** I like the game Everybody Who, where students are seated in a circle and then have to stand up, high-five someone else standing, and switch places when you call out an attribute they identify with (e.g., "Everybody who likes video games!")

- **Each week, as a daily warm up, ask the class questions to identify a handful of their classmates.** These questions should be about strengths, interests, or positive contributions to the class: e.g., "Who held the door for everyone when we were in the library? Hint: they also really like Oreos!" Give students who identify their classmate a prize or special privilege, and vary the students each week.
- **Have students share each week, either verbally or in a Ticket Out the Door, how someone else was kind to them.** This practice will help everyone's brains to notice kindness when it happens. For students with autism who may be pre-disposed to focus on the negatives, this can help to nurture a positive mindset and sense of belonging in school. Keep track of who they think has been kind to them. This may help you design groups later!
- **Consider having special weeks throughout the year where students draw names and must make an effort to be kind to that person** by putting up their chair at the end of the day, saying hello, asking them to join, etc. Challenge them to keep it secret, if they can. This can be linked to a language response in which they write what it felt like to be kind and to receive kindness.
- **If students are seated in groups, give them time to come up with a fun group name you can call them by.** Build their sense of togetherness. Use positive classroom motivation, like rewarding the desk groups when you notice students doing well. You can point out when these positives are because of your student with autism or simply catch kids being kind: "I loved how Johnny got out his materials and was ready. You too, Suzy. This group is all ready, wow!" Do not, however, do the opposite and take away privileges or points "because Johnny wasn't listening" and risk having peers turn on that child. Instead, use friendly reminders yourself: "I want everyone to be showing whole-body listening…"; then give them the chance to process and follow through.
- **Find ways to highlight the strengths of autistic students so peers see what they have to offer.** This could be through special projects, having them teach the class a topic they are experts in, or even having Dare to Share Time, where they and other classmates can present a favorite item, joke, or success to the class. Ask audience members to practice making a positive comment, asking a question to show interest, or making a personal connection in response to these presentations.

5

Connecting the Pieces

> **Puzzling Out the Big Picture**
>
> I once dumped a 48-piece puzzle in front of my students without showing them the box first. "Put it together," I instructed. And then I watched. There were four students in total, ages 12 and 13. They all had autism and two were also in gifted education classes. I wondered how they would go about approaching this challenge.
>
> You might be thinking how you'd go about a similar task. Perhaps you'd sort the larger pile into smaller piles organized by color. Maybe you'd pick out all the edge pieces and start laying out the frame. My students did not possess any inherent strategy except for trial and error. They would each pick up two pieces to see if they fit together; if they did not, they'd drop both pieces back in the massive pile of pieces. I watched for several nail-biting minutes before I broke down and suggested they look for border pieces. They responded in much the same way: scavenging for two border pieces, seeing if they fit, and, if not, dropping them back in the pile.

This task revealed several cognitive traits of students with autism: a tendency to focus on the details, rather than the main idea; and difficulty planning, organizing, and thinking flexibly in order to problem-solve or achieve a goal. There are multiple theories that attempt to explain some of the information processing difficulties experienced by people with autism. We've already discussed theory of mind, context-blindness, and difficulties with generalizing from a social lens. In this chapter, we'll look at some of the other theories to explain how our students approach learning and assessments.

Information Processing

Weak Central Coherence

We often use language to focus on weaknesses instead of strengths when talking about autism. Weak central coherence is a heritable trait found in many people with and without autism, and can be an asset in many fields, including law, engineering, medicine, academia, and any job that requires a keen eye for details (Happé & Frith, 2006). It could be the reason why, when everyone else was focusing on the plot of an episode of *Tom and Jerry* in which the cartoon characters wear swimming trunks at the beach, one of my students looked at his parents in shock and said, "So all this time, they've been running around naked?" That detail was overlooked by everyone else, and was perhaps not the most important detail in the grand scheme of things, but a good point nonetheless!

Since first suggesting weak central coherence in 1989, Frith has refined this idea to mean a thinking style that shows preference for local processing of information over global processing. Yeah, yeah, but what does that really mean? Various studies have shown that many autistic individuals do not synthesize different pieces of information to get to the gist (Pellicano, 2010; Plaisted, 2001); in essence, their often detailed-oriented strengths mean they can overlook the bigger picture. This can be the case in visual spatial tasks as well as language tasks, where they may be excellent word decoders, but fail to use context to read for meaning (Pellicano, 2010; Vanegas & Davidson, 2014). There is also evidence that some people with autism have trouble recognizing faces, which may be related to weak central coherence (López et al., 2004). I have had several students who have trouble recognizing me when a significant feature changes, such as when I wear my glasses (rare), when I cut my hair so that I have bangs, or when I dye my otherwise translucent eyebrows a dark color! Perhaps they are focusing on the details rather than the whole picture, or perhaps they are unnerved by something that should be predictable suddenly seeming not so predictable.

There is some debate about whether weak central coherence is a symptom or a cause, whether it is the result of specific brain mechanisms, who on the spectrum are affected by it, and in what situations it manifests (Brock & Bzishvili, 2013; Burnette et al., 2005). Research is mixed. Not everyone with autism demonstrates weak central coherence (Burnette et al., 2005; Vermeulen, 2012), which may just be natural variation in skills. Other explanations put forward to explain weak central coherence include brain underconnectivity, which makes it difficult for the brain to process information when different areas of the brain need to work together (Just et al., 2004), as well as difficulties with generalization (Ch. 2), as people with autism may focus on irrelevant details or on details that are different rather than similar, which makes it difficult to see what is in common between concepts or situations in order to make sense of an experience and build new knowledge (Plaisted, 2001). Whatever the cause, autistic folks have more difficulty knowing what's important to focus on if they are not told.

It is essential for us, as teachers, to understand this: autistic people can use global processing when they are explicitly cued to do so (López et al., 2004; Plaisted, 2001; Happé & Frith, 2006). So they may default to processing information in separate bits, but can change processes when it is required. Telling them how to approach a task levels the playing field so that they can perform as well as their peers. If they are not identifying the main idea, we can draw their attention to it. If they don't know what a question is getting at, we can be more specific or show them how to highlight what it is really asking. We can also enjoy the unique conclusions they may come to—just because their lens focuses on something different, it doesn't mean it's wrong or irrelevant!

Executive Dysfunction

Executive function skills essentially help us to self-regulate in order to achieve a future goal (Barkley, 2016). If you ever took Psychology 101, you probably learned about the Marshmallow Test, which presents children with a marshmallow and tells them if they can wait to eat it, they will be given another marshmallow.

Many things in life benefit us more in the long run if we can delay gratification and manage our emotions while we wait. This is part of executive functioning (Barkley, 2016; Center on the Developing Child, 2011). Executive function also includes emotional regulation, which we will talk about in Chapter 6. Research is mixed on all the sub-skills included as part of executive functioning, but it is generally agreed that it includes

1. Working memory: the ability to keep in mind and use newly learned information in the immediate context, such as instructions or new concepts
2. Inhibition: the ability to filter our thoughts, actions, and distractions so that we can attend to what is important
3. Cognitive flexibility: the ability to plan, revise the plan, incorporate new information, problem-solve, and adapt to new demands (Barkley, 2016; Center on the Developing Child, 2011; Tranter & Kerr, 2016).

Executive dysfunction affects people with attention deficit hyperactivity disorder (ADHD) or autism and it can also present in someone who experienced childhood trauma or adverse childhood experiences, or who was raised in unpredictable environments (Center on the Developing Child, 2011). As any teacher knows, some of our students with executive dysfunction are a whirlwind of activity, needing constant stimulation and seeing everything but what you want them to be noticing. Others have a complete lack of energy, with their heads on their desk and sluggish movements when asked to transition. Some children display both characteristics at different times (Tranter & Kerr, 2016). These individuals have nervous systems that react differently from those of others. They may display a fight-or-flight response to a demand that doesn't seem stressful to others and, later, may go into a rest-and-digest mode (Tranter & Kerr, 2016). Many of these children have social difficulties as well, and many do not outgrow their executive function difficulties (Center on the Developing Child, 2011). A child's executive functioning in preschool directly predicts their future academic success and readiness (Center on the Developing Child, 2011; Pellicano, 2012).

In the classroom, executive function skills are responsible for how well a child sits, listens, participates appropriately, reads, writes, remembers task instructions, works independently, organizes materials, keeps track of time, manages group demands, plays, (Barkley, 2016; Center on the Developing Child, 2011; Pellicano, 2012)—I could go on! Pretty much all the skills we want students to have to be successful in school are in some way linked to executive function. At home, there are not the same demands, so teachers are often the first to notice that kids with executive function challenges are not developing as expected (Center on the Developing Child, 2011). Executive function skills can develop through children's play, so it makes sense that this might be impaired in autistic or other socially vulnerable children (Center on the Developing Child, 2011). The demands on their executive functioning increase with age and, so, middle school tends to be harder for kids with ADHD or autism, which affects their self-esteem, and their social and academic performance (Attwood, 2007; Murphy, 2011).

There isn't a ton of research specific to kids with high-functioning autism and what their real-life executive function challenges look like (Pellicano, 2010; Pugliese et al., 2016; Rosenthal et al., 2013). What comes to mind for me is a student who, when packing his backpack each day, spreads his books and materials all over the classroom floor to make sure he has everything, taking significantly longer than his classmates and often leaving long after the bell rings. He just can't organize in an efficient manner or see what needs to be done. Research shows that autistic children tend to experience greater difficulty with executive function requirements as they age (Channon et al., 2001; Pugliese et al., 2016; Rosenthal et al., 2013; Vanegas & Davidson, 2014). While intelligence is a predictor of future independence in typically developing children, this isn't the case for kids with autism. Rather, their executive functioning and ability to self-monitor are better predictors of their future adaptive skills (Pugliese et al., 2016).

In Channon and colleagues' 2001 study of the problem-solving abilities of teens with Asperger Syndrome, they were found to have significant difficulty remembering relevant details, generating high-quality solutions, and selecting the most beneficial solutions. Though the number of solutions they generated was similar to the typically developing control group, often their suggestions were not socially appropriate or were unrealistic. In a different task, they were presented with a new problem and a list of possible solutions, and were able to rank solutions from most likely to be effective to least likely to be effective in a similar manner to their peers. Their performance on these two tasks makes sense if we consider both executive functioning and weak central coherence. When structure was provided and solutions were pre-generated, they had an easier time. However, when asked to solve a problem without any guidance, they seemed to demonstrate difficulty zeroing in on what is important, planning, and evaluating the long-term potential of the plan. In real-life scenarios, this must be even more difficult! I have heard countless times from parents that their child goes home and reveals major problems that occurred during the day, without having ever brought it to a teacher's attention! One of my students went to the washroom during a group work period and then did not know how to rejoin his group, and so sat at his desk when he returned, without a word to anyone. My brother Danny has a job shredding documents at an office and once shredded his pay because his piggy bank was full! All of these are examples of how people with autism are not likely to turn to others for help, and their dilemmas can be invisible to those around them.

Research suggests executive functioning and weak central coherence are independent processes (Happé & Frith, 2006; Pellicano, 2010). The way I see it, both contribute to a difficulty with recognizing and attending to what others deem important. Like other cognitive differences that are symptomatic of autism, these processing differences vary in intensity across individuals with (and without) autism (Happé & Frith, 2006). I've had students with exceptional organization skills (often to a rigid degree) who cannot cope if their writing looks less than perfect, and also students who are very cognitively flexible but who are walking tornadoes. Some students have had highly developed work habits but were resistant to feedback once something was on paper, while others have needed prompts for each step but have had a beautiful ability to think outside the box. Like every growing human in our care, their strengths and weaknesses are unique to them. This brings us back to an essential truth: we must *know* each student.

Language Processing

My brother Danny is a master of wordplay and has a quip for everything. He's hilarious. His often sophisticated use of language means those who don't know him well might be taken aback when he walks away, wordlessly, if asked too many questions at one time. It's surprising that we forget to consider language difficulties experienced by autistic children who are very verbal and with average-to-gifted intellectual abilities. Their language differences are easy to overlook, often masked by their large vocabularies, factual knowledge, and keen interest in grammar and spelling. Instead, people with autism struggle with pragmatic language (Attwood, 2007; Lartseva et al., 2015). Pragmatics include all the other ways we communicate and interpret meaning, including figurative language, nonverbal cues, context, and prior knowledge. Essentially, they have difficulty with the underlying message of what others communicate (Frith, 1989).

Their tendency to be blind to context in social situations also spills over into language processing. Homographs are words that are spelled the same but have different meanings; they may be pronounced differently, such as "the nurse *wound* the bandage around the *wound*." Studies show that children with autism do not use context to determine the correct pronunciation of homographs (Frith & Snowling, 1983; Happé, 1997), with 75% showing weak central coherence when processing sentences, focusing on the more immediate word rather than the sentence meaning as a whole, and so tending to complete a sentence with an unusual suggestion, such as "Hens lay eggs and *bacon*." This was not seen in neurotypical peers or in children with ADHD (Booth & Happé, 2010). Another study showed that, once autistic folks learn idioms, they default to that learned figurative meaning even if the expression was actually meant literally; for example, if presented with the term "it's a piece of cake" when there is a slice of dessert offered (Le Sourn-Bissaoui et al., 2011), having difficulty using context or perspective-taking to see how two possible meanings might apply.

We also know that autistic people process language in different areas of the brain and these areas do not work in a synchronized fashion (Just et al., 2004). This enhanced local processing means they spend a significant amount of brainpower uncovering the meaning of individual words (Just et al., 2004; Koolen et al., 2012). With all their energy focused on low-level tasks, it makes sense that it's harder for them to keep other information in mind. Their working memory can also be affected, meaning they might find it hard to remember and follow instructions, understand the meaning of text or spoken directions, and learn new concepts (Murphy, 2014).

Executive function is also tied to reading and writing abilities. Generating ideas, planning, and organizing ideas on the page are difficult tasks for children with executive dysfunction (Murphy, 2011). In children with autism, it is even more difficult to keep in mind the perspective of someone reading their work and to communicate with intent. Reading is all about getting to the gist, which

---

I was reminded of this recently when a student brought up the game of pool. Together, he and I tried to explain how the game worked to other students. We described the table, covered in green felt with deep pockets in each corner, the balls (stripes and solids), and the elements of game play, using pencils to mime how to use a pool cue. After all this, another student told me she was confused and thought we were talking about a swimming pool. Her fantastic advice was we should have pulled up a picture so she could visualize the difference.

What working memory looks like in typical learners (list on the left) and with executive dysfunction (lists on the right) (adapted from S. Murphy)

People with autism can have issues processing speech in noisy contexts (Mamashli, 2017) and have greater difficulty processing auditory information than visual information (see review by Lartseva et al., 2015). I was stunned when one of my students shared that he needs closed captioning on when watching videos or it all sounds like the Charlie Brown teacher voice (i.e., gibberish!) to him.

can be a challenge for kids who focus more on the words individually than as a whole. Research suggests children with autism also use less mental imagery when processing sentences (Just et al., 2004). Executive dysfunction can cause children to be easily distracted by other things happening in the room, which can mean they miss out during silent reading and read-alouds, and are likely to forget what they've read (Murphy, 2011).

Teaching Strategies

So that's the theory. The problem with most research is that it is conducted in tightly controlled environments that aren't an accurate reflection of what happens in day-to-day life. So, what are some practices that support our students in real classrooms? What does all of this mean for how we teach?

Say What You Mean and Mean What You Say

Perhaps the most important part of connecting with kids with autism, and connecting them to others, is being someone they can trust. The more approachable and predictable you can be, the better (Vermeulen, 2012). Think of it this way: if other people were not predictable to you, and the world seemed to be governed not by logic but by magic with things seeming to happen out of nowhere (Sinha et al., 2014), you'd want a Gandalf by your side. You'd want a reliable sage to guide you, whose reactions could keep you grounded. You'd want someone who could explain what to do when you needed to hear it. In fact, developing executive functioning is reliant on strong adult models (Center on the Developing Child, 2011; Tranter & Kerr, 2016). Here are some tips:

- **Give clear instructions, one step at a time.** Try to clear background noise and distractions so that it's easier for kids with autism to pay attention to what's important.
- **Visuals matter.** Write down instructions and help to reduce working memory load (Barkley, 2016). Remember, difficulties with working memory are not the same as factual memory (Barkley, 2016). I've had students who could recall the exact date I said something, but who could not hold more than a step or two of instructions in their head at a time.
- **Show what success looks like.** Use exemplars, not only of the end process, but of each component of an assignment.
- **Explain the purpose of tasks.** Help them to connect the pieces. This will help them understand why they're expected to do the work.
- **Build feedback into the process.** Let them know work is not complete without a review and possible revisions. Your feedback, in particular, is important because you are the one marking the work, and whose perspective they need to take!
- **Do not promise—or threaten—something you will not be able to follow through on.** They will remember and hold you to it. One of my students would become agitated if he so much as lost a pencil because his parent had told him if he didn't do well at school, he'd break his video games. This threat stayed with him and caused him to have more anxiety and behaviors than if another approach had been used. Kids with autism expect you to keep your word, for better or for worse. Choose your words carefully.

- **Always follow through on what you say.** There are times you might have to delay following through on a class party or reward, and so make your apologies and give the reason why. Let them know when it will be happening instead.
- **Explain figurative language.** We use figurative language all the time, so when you catch yourself using an expression that could be hard for literal thinkers to understand, comment on it and reduce their confusion. I'll never forget a student who was clutching his ear during a lesson because, "My mom says when I'm listening everything goes right through and out my other ear, so I am trying to keep it all inside my brain!"
- **Teach them to self-advocate and that you will listen.** Turn your whole body to face them and help them to problem-solve their concerns.
- **Acknowledge efforts.** They so often hear about what they're not doing, make a point of praising them when you see them following routines or taking greater steps toward independence on their own.

Help to Pinpoint What's Important

Regardless of cognitive theory, children with autism might have difficulty attending to what is important but are able to do it when explicitly cued. This gives us a lot of direction for how to teach. We must activate context before we expect them to tune into it (Vermeulen, 2012). If we draw their attention to consider what a person might be thinking, language being used figuratively, or what is expected in a situation, their minds attend, with conscious effort, to those details. This processing doesn't happen spontaneously or in the background, and may not happen in real-time interactions without a prompt. It's as if their minds can't differentiate what is important unless we tell them where to look. It reminds me of the time 40 autistic children were asked to share what they were looking forward to on our upcoming camp trip. Each student began to share: "S'mores!" "Being away from home!" "Going on the giant swing!" The teacher leading the activity prompted the next student, "What are you looking forward to?"

"Going to Value Village!"

Despite the fact 30 other kids had stayed on a specific topic, this student hadn't picked up on the trend. My word to the wise: teach the processes you wish to see with the following provisos:

- **Inferencing** is difficult, especially for perfectionists who worry about making mistakes. Students with autism are not usually well-practiced at getting to the main idea; understanding cause and effect; identifying bias, purpose, or audience; or making predictions. It's not that they can't; it's that we may need to teach them how to do it and what details are relevant to make a judgment. When reading, you might want to model the process or have them highlight what is important so they see it visually. You might need to ask questions to activate their background knowledge. Ask them what details they've learned about specific characters and what that has taught us about the character. Get them thinking about the main idea. Before I show a video, I prime students by telling them what I want them to look out for in the video, and what question I will ask them after the video is done. When I first start asking students to identify the message of a text, video, or song, I remind them that this is not always a plot point or the title, but rather an unstated message for the readers that says something about our relationship to others or to the world around us. For a few sessions I will prompt, "What is this fable telling us about how we should treat others?" or "What does this teach us about being a part of a community?" Eventually, I'll fade the questions that tell them what to attend to and will see how they fare if I simply ask, "What is the message?"

- **Distilling information** can be a challenge. It's hard to zero in on the most important facts; summarize a book or movie; take notes without stressing about writing every word uttered; provide just the right amount of background information when speaking; or create a title that encapsulates the content of an essay. I once got an email from a student, the subject line of which read: "READ THE EMAIL." Ask the class to develop a summary together and write down the important points they identify (and talk through what is not so important if there is any confusion). Generate title ideas after reading a numbered chapter together. Ask students to summarize what they just read or learned to a partner. Provide organizers or fill-in-the-blank notes to help them look for specific information to fill in during lessons. Have them draw pictures of the main idea of lessons.

Samples of Language Organizers

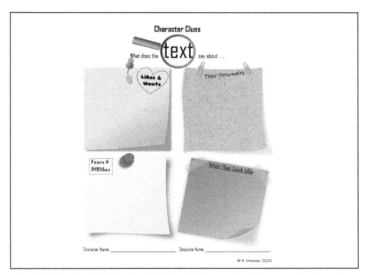

- **Set parameters for open-ended tasks**. That first-day activity where you have students *Write about your favorite part of the summer* may have them wracking their brains for hours, trying to figure out exactly which part was, in fact, their favorite. A better question might be *Write about an activity you enjoyed this*

Teaching Strategies 69

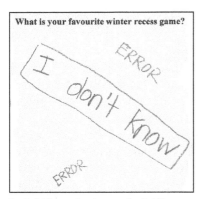

I might have had more luck if I asked, "What is one winter recess game you enjoy?"

summer, or you might present two or three choices of specific writing prompts. One of my students was asked to write about an overnight trip and wrote a 20-page essay, going into the minutiae of what was served at each meal, every point on the itinerary, and what times he woke and went to sleep. Had he been prompted to write about three things he enjoyed, he may have had an easier time! Because he didn't know what information the teacher was looking for, he compensated by including all of it.

- **Teach students to verbalize**, talking through steps they need to take quietly under their breath. Research shows children with autism don't use verbal rehearsal strategies (see review of Pellicano, 2010). Speaking as they read can also help with reading comprehension, as it gives them another modality through which to process the text (Murphy, 2011).

- **Engage imaginative strengths.** Prompt them to imagine texts read aloud as a "movie in their minds." Many years ago I began incorporating highly imaginative guided meditations into our day. During them, I would briefly pause so students could explore a vista in their minds and share about it. Students who generally had difficulties focusing told the most incredible stories about their adventures! Their imaginations and memories were fantastic, and I began to wonder if I could harness those abilities at other times. I started reminding them that read-alouds were just like meditations, where you pictured what was happening like a movie in your mind. Suddenly, these students were able to answer questions if I stopped mid-text. They were engaged and following along significantly more often! It was incredible to see that a simple prompt (and some practice of the skill) unlocked the door for them to better access the text.

- **Teach note-taking and offer different levels of organizers.**
  Level 1, Most Support: Provide full notes and have them highlight what's important. Teach the whole class how to summarize notes by using a code in the margin for items to remember for tests (e.g., D=Date; P=Person of Note) and using symbols like arrows to show causal relationships. I also encourage drawing simple emoticons to show feelings of people affected by historical events.
  Level 2, Some Support: Provide fill-in-the-blank notes to reduce the writing requirement and increase on-task engagement. Remind students to code their notes, as they go or after, for homework.
  Level 3, Independent: Provide a blank organizer for students to take their own notes and code later.

Sample of a Level 1 history organizer filled in by student (left); sample of a Level 2 history organizer as presented by teacher (right). See page 78 for Level 3 History Organizer template.

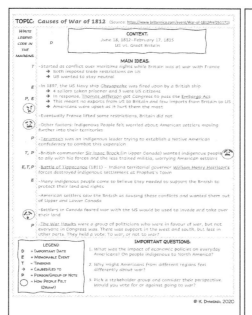

See page 79 for a History Study Guide template.

- **Teach how to study from notes.** Give students time to transfer coded notes to a summary document to help them to study. As they do this, they can also jot down any questions they still have. Once finished, have them plan how they will answer those questions and record their responses. They can also use these documents to quiz classmates!

Teaching Strategies   71

Planning and Organization

There is a certain irony that I teach physical organization to students, because I have always had a messy desk and, once, tearing apart the house looking for my keys, I found them in the refrigerator. Students with autism are more than just physically disorganized; they also have trouble being aware of their own thoughts, organizing them, and monitoring their own progress. Like other students with executive function challenges, they may not be aware of time passing or how much time to allot certain tasks. They are very much in the moment. Interestingly, while their peers can use more mental energy during difficult tasks, autistic students have brains that approach all tasks as equally taxing, using up significant mental resources even for simple tasks (Mamashli, 2017). How exhausting! They need to be directly taught how to plan and approach tasks, and can benefit from adults taking on the role of "surrogate executive functioning" (Murphy, 2011). So how do we help them plan?

Awareness of Time

- **Use sub-tasks.** Break down tasks for them so that they do not feel overwhelmed at the sheer amount that needs to be done. Many of my students have an all-or-nothing approach; they have to be taught that projects are a process, not meant to be done in one sitting, but tackled a little bit each day. Tell them explicitly what parts to do when. I've seen teachers use incredible strategies, such as giving students a duotang with one step of the project listed per page instead of a master to-do list. Another teacher painted her students' desks with a whiteboard coating and had them write their own checklist for a work period on their desk. Low-tech options include writing a step or two on a sticky note and giving it to the student, checking in, and then assigning the next portion for completion.
- **Ask students to tell you what they need to do next.** You can also teach students to repeat instructions to themselves and use self-talk to engage with tasks before seeking reassurance. Self-talk is another way executive function develops, and children with autism are less likely to verbally rehearse tasks (Pellicano, 2012).
- **Time transitions.** Let them know how much time is left in a work period. I give ten-minute, five-minute, two-minute, and "finish your sentence and then begin putting away materials" reminders.
- **Visual countdown aids** can help them to see the time remaining. Sometimes, students can become frazzled by the time crunch if they feel they should have finished work by the end of the period. You can reassure them that not finishing is okay and give them options of how and when to finish the task.
- **Teach how to prioritize.** Have two sections to your homework board: *Due Tomorrow* and *Due Later*. If they need it, help them write out what to do and when in their agendas, particularly for larger tasks or studying (e.g., "Study p. 2 on Monday, and p. 3 on Tuesday").
- **Introduce a fun challenge.** If students are heel-draggers when packing their bag or getting ready to leave, time them. Make a game out of beating their time each day.

Managing Materials

- **Color code materials by subject.**

> I never expect them to stop immediately or unexpectedly. Transitioning gently is equally important for preferred and less-preferred tasks; I'd be pretty annoyed if someone demanded without warning that I turn off the TV during an episode of *Grey's Anatomy*!

- **Teach *a place for everything*!** When we start the year teaching routines and expectations for where things go and how to use them, we save ourselves a lot of headaches and reminders later.
- **Show visuals of what to take out.** Ask students what they think they need to have out on their desks and what they can do if they don't know. Students with autism might not realize they can ask someone or look around to see what others have out. If possible, take photos of common classroom materials (e.g., math textbook and notebook) and print them out on magnets or laminate them. Have students help you put them up on the board at the beginning of a class as a reference. You can also hold up the items.
- **Set times for organizational tasks,** such as cleaning out desks or filing loose papers. If it's not possible to do this as a class, remind students that part of the routine includes using any extra time after work is finished for these important tasks.
- **Teach the hidden curriculum of organization.** Once a desk is clean, remind them that when they put away work they should physically look inside and ensure they are placing things neatly. My rules: books/textbooks on one side; notebooks, duotangs, and paper on the other; organized from smallest on top to largest on the bottom so you can always see what's inside.
- **Find out their preference for filing loose sheets.** Loose papers can be hard to file. Many autistic children have fine and gross motor difficulties, making it hard to use a binder or duotang. Pocket folders can be effective. Some students need a transitional folder to store loose sheets to file at another time. Have them test options to decide what feels comfortable.
- **Consider alternative storing arrangements,** such as a magazine rack, bin, or shelf area, if they are having difficulty managing space in the desk. Give them specific rules to follow, not just more space in which to be disorganized.
- **Give extra time to pack bags.** Some students benefit from having a set time in the morning to pack their bags, in addition to the usual end-of-day time. Visuals of what needs to be packed can help students to not leave water bottles, lunch bags, or other items behind.
- **Give extra space to pack bags.** Sometimes students struggle to pack bags at the bag hook area, surrounded by 25 bodies all bumping into one another. Consider allowing an autistic student to get their bag and bring it to their desk to pack before the rest of the class rushes over.

Organizing Ideas

- **Reduce the writing requirement when not assessing writing!** They are more likely to get ideas on paper if you provide visual organizers, fill-in-the-blank worksheets, and other formats.
- **Give specific details about your writing expectations.** If they aren't meeting your expectations, tell them what you want to see.
- **Have students tell partners what they plan to write** before a writing period.
- **Teach them how to brainstorm before writing down ideas.** Show examples of alternative formats and ask their preference; for example, visual mind mapping or writing down point-form notes.
- **Descriptive feedback** back and forth between teacher and students gives them individualized responses so they know what you're looking for and helps them to view writing as a process.
- **Let them know if they need to explain their thinking or include more (or less) background information.** They may need help with this when speaking,

> One student I taught used to loop sentences when writing. We began looking at her work as a first draft, highlighting the important ideas, and then she would rewrite without the looped thoughts. She is now able to write coherent journal entries on her own.

too. One of my students gives very lo-o-o-o-ong stories as answers, both orally and in writing. At first, I talked privately with her about extraneous details and which were the salient points. I suggested a shorter way she could have made the same great connection for greater impact. Then I'd have her suggest the "movie trailer version" instead of doing it for her. Now her answers are much more concise and to-the-point!

Structure for Success

One thing I've learned, whether teaching Grade 1, Grade 5, Grade 7, or adults in teacher education: everyone benefits from explicit teaching and setting the framework early. Teach the routines you want students to follow. When you scaffold activities, you are teaching the routines and structure you want students to use and, over time, you can back away. They are developing their executive functioning skills and ability to manage on their own (Center on the Developing Child, 2011). Here are some things to keep in mind when planning to teach:

Intentional Instruction

- **Balance activities throughout the day**. Students with executive dysfunction get very tired in the afternoon and may find tasks involving too much writing or group work very tough. When I plan, I vary how students are producing responses. For some lessons, we have discussions. Then students might produce a comic strip, diagram, or other visual representation that uses words but is more likely to sustain their interests. Videos help to teach core concepts and seem to stick better in their memories; they make a good lesson hook and are especially helpful in engaging students in the afternoons. I also make sure we're getting up and role playing or engaging in hands-on activities at least one lesson a day. I want them to be comfortable producing their knowledge in different ways, and it gives me a sense of what situations help them to shine. I make sure something highly preferred is scheduled after something less fun, so that natural breaks and rewards are built into the day.
- **Consider pacing and how you balance information delivery throughout the day**. Try not to lecture at break-neck speed or give too much information all at once.
- **Reduce their mental workload**. Visuals help them understand what you mean. Organizers help focus their attention. Written and visual instructions mean they don't have to rely on working memory. Giving them breaks helps free up mental energy. Remember, all the demands on their executive functioning depletes their neural resources (Barkley, 2016). These are all strategies that help level the playing field.
- **Give them processing time.** I am super comfortable, now, with asking my class a question and saying, "I'm going to wait a moment to give everyone a chance to think and respond." This helps me ensure I'm hearing from more students, not just the ones who raise their hand the fastest. I don't do this for every question I ask but, just like calling on a specific student to answer, it's a tool I use sometimes.
- **Use visual aids,** like manipulatives, so students can see relationships between concepts and access learning through different modalities.
- **Prompt as needed.** Remember, they won't always pick up on subtle group reminders (Barkley, 2016) and might need a personal reminder. The goal, ultimately, is to teach the skills they need to approach current and future tasks.

When you must prompt, change it up. Sometimes it can be repetition of instructions. Sometimes ask them what they need to do next. Sometimes you can point to the visuals or steps, reducing verbal input and possible prompt dependence.

Work Periods

- **Chunk and check in.** Some students might need you to give them a few questions or parts of a task at a time. See that they know what to do, and then give them the space to try on their own and build independence. Consider cutting up worksheets into strips or asking them how many questions they can do, and reducing work to what's essential (Barkley, 2016). Increase the number of questions as they become more confident with autonomous work.
- **Allow movement breaks.** Students might need sensory input to be able to focus. You can teach them when different options are appropriate. For instance, it's expected to sit during instructional time and use a quiet, non-distracting fidget object that allows their eyes to be looking toward the front, like a squeeze ball or a piece of Velcro taped inside the desk so they can feel the texture. They are free to take a brief walk or stretch break during work periods, and can sit, stand, or move to another area of the class to produce work.
- **Make work periods enjoyable.** Play music quietly during work periods or allow students to listen to music on headphones.

Homework

- **Reduce (or eliminate) homework.** Studying and working on projects over a longer period but in shorter time increments each day is a good habit to develop. Page after page of math or language is not going to stick. Students with autism have used up all their effort, attention, and neural energy on the sheer amount of processing required of them at school and in social situations. For any child with executive dysfunction, they need a break to regenerate (Barkley, 2016). However, if they are not using their schoolwork periods at all, unfinished work might need to go home.
- **Communication with parents/guardians is key.** You might need to combine forces with parents to have a reward system for work completion in class, if it remains an ongoing problem. Parents might also want work sent home to reinforce what is being taught in the classroom. Suggest videos of concepts instead of written work. Remind parents they do not have to "take up" work but just do a completion check so that their child can participate in the experience of the class taking up and correcting work.
- **Support agenda writing.** I've taught my students they can write agendas in code, by making a legend (e.g., M = Math, L = Language). This way, they can simplify what needs to be copied down. Some students benefit from a homework checklist, where the subjects and materials are prewritten and just need to be circled and the relevant pages and numbers written in. Even better, using an online platform where a photo of the homework board is posted that parents can also see eliminates the need for the end-of-day routine. One of my students relished the job of taking the photo for the class and posting it to the class website!

Assessments

- **Assess in ways that benefit your students.** Most of my students do a better job explaining their thinking orally. Some shine when they can draw and write a

Teaching Strategies 75

short amount to explain their thinking. When you can, vary assessment tasks. Special-interest projects often are great entry points to the curriculum for kids with executive dysfunction.

- **Review rubric criteria as a class.** Present work samples at various levels and have students discuss and grade the samples. Then, after students have completed their assignments, have them self- and peer-assess on the rubric before considering their final product complete. You might also want students to complete a final assessment and reward them for accuracy if their marks match yours (Barkley, 2016).
- **Tell them what to study.** Just as we give students specific criteria for assignments, kids with autism need to know what's important to study. You can help reduce test anxiety by telling them specifically what kinds of questions/topics will be on the tests. Other students can figure this out, as they intuitively sense what is most important. Because autistic kids focus on details and not the whole picture, they don't know where to focus their energy.
- **Consider how work or tests look on paper.** Too many words or questions, or not enough space, can be visually overwhelming.
- **Ask yourself if assessment questions are easy to read.** They might notice only the first or last part of a wordy or multi-step question. It can be helpful to redesign a worksheet or test so that it is clearly broken down in steps, with lots of white space.
- **Ask yourself if assessment questions are easy to respond to.** Avoid compound questions that could present a dilemma: *What to answer first?* Just ask two separate questions instead! Keep in mind that kids with autism have more trouble communicating how they know something, and that they might fare better if given true or false statements, multiple choice, or circle-the-correct-answer options.
- **Use your autism lens to double-check how you word test questions,** as these students might take you very literally. They will not necessarily see the gist of a question. Be sure your question is asking what you want it to ask. How many facts do you want for the answer to be a substantial answer? Why not tell them "include at least three examples"? Set them up for success!

When I asked students what they wanted to be as adults, I received some conventional—and less conventional—answers. I didn't specify careers, after all!

76 *Connecting the Pieces*

- **Don't demand too much memorization.** If it's possible, let them have a reference for math formulas or other concepts. Let them use calculators and other learning aids that reduce working memory load.
- **Give them "Time off the Clock"** (Barkley, 2016). Kids with executive dysfunction don't necessarily need significantly more time on tests, but they perform better when able to pause, take movement or stretch breaks, and then resume without time penalties. This strategy gives them the chance to refocus and reset their thinking, rather than just giving them more time in which to be unfocused.

History Organizer

TOPIC:

Write legend code in the margins.

CONTEXT:

MAIN IDEAS:

IMPORTANT QUESTIONS:

LEGEND
- D = Important Date
- E = Memorable Event
- T = Tensions
- → = Caused/Led to
- P = Person/Group of Note
- O = How People Felt (Draw!)

History Study Guide

TOPIC:	
IMPORTANT DATES	
MEMORABLE EVENTS	
TENSIONS	
CAUSES & EFFECTS	
PEOPLE OF NOTE	
HOW PEOPLE FELT	
QUESTIONS I STILL HAVE:	
MY PLAN TO FIND THE ANSWERS:	
WHAT I LEARNED:	

Pembroke Publishers ©2020 *The Autism Lens* by Kara Dymond ISBN 978-1-55138-347-7

6

Connecting Sensory, Anxiety, and Emotional Regulation

At least a few times a year, Sonia and I hear comments like this: "You're not a REAL teacher. You don't yell at us and you're fun. You listen." "You seem nice so far. But will you be one of those teachers who yells at me later?"

I often have to explain to students how tough it is to manage a classroom. Still, it's important for teachers to recognize how our volume can affect children with autism. Recently my classes contributed tips for teachers for a video created for a workshop. Almost all my 18 students said, "Don't yell!" I had to start prompting them to think of different examples! It makes me sad, sometimes, how much my students feel the adults in their lives scold and discipline them. The problem of a raised voice isn't just the big feelings it evokes; it's the fact that autistic folks might experience their senses more intensely than others. In fact, their brain waves respond differently than those of their peers when they hear angry intonation (Korpilahti et al., 2007). That raised voice that gets the attention of other students because it's mildly annoying can be physically painful to students with autism. Which, of course, raises their anxiety... Which could then increase behaviors others find challenging.

Sensory Processing

It's impossible to talk about autism without acknowledging sensory differences. Not only are they part of the diagnosis for people with autism (APA, 2013), sensory differences also fundamentally alter their experience of the world. Two studies conducted by Leekham and colleagues (2007) showed that 90% of all children on the autism spectrum are affected by sensory symptoms across multiple sensory domains. This was found to be true for all autistic children, regardless of age or cognitive ability.

In Chapter 3, we learned about predictive thinking and how neurotypical brains save time and processing power by comparing reality to a predicted schema of what is expected in any given situation. Predictability means less processing work for the neurotypical brain, as it maximizes efficiency by filtering what they attend to and enabling quick recognition (Vermeulen, 2012). This is why, when we go to the mall intent only on getting a teal raincoat, we scan and notice things that are blue, green, and teal, ignoring much of the rest. It's why, when I'm driving and a passenger says, "Wow, did you see that other driver who was eating a candy bar?" my answer is usually no. My brain helps me to ignore extraneous details so I can attend to the relevant details when driving from point A to point B. Almost like magic, my brain can figure out what is important and what is not, and saves me brainpower by not processing everything around me. I miss a lot of things.

Many people with autism seem to notice everything. Sometimes their sensory differences can be an asset, like giving the individual perfect pitch (Miller, 1999 as cited by Happé & Frith, 2006) or the increased perceptual capacity to detect auditory differences that go undetected by others. In the research of Remington and Fairnie (2017), autistic folks outperformed the control group as the auditory load of a listening task increased. They were asked to pay attention to a recorded conversation of two women so they could answer a subsequent question. Partway through, a male voice interjected, "I'm a gorilla." Almost 50% of autistic participants picked up on this, compared to 12% of neurotypical participants.

The flipside of the coin, of course, is that when they aren't given a specific task to attend to, or when something isn't predictable, the brains of people with autism have to process all the peripheral information, which can result in not focusing on what is deemed important by others (Remington & Fairnie, 2017). Predictability plays a large part in how they might react, which explains why a student terrified of the noise of a fire alarm can blast their own music over their headphones. They know when to expect it and what it will sound like. When they don't know, they could have an extremely negative response to different sensory experiences, characterized by fear, distress, or pain (Green et al., 2013; Happé & Frith, 2006; MacLennan et al., 2020). Almost 80% of autistic children are hypersensitive to sounds, smells, or light, while 70% are hypersensitive to touch and to certain food tastes and textures (Mayes et al., 2012). Hypersensitivity can manifest as a shock or as pain from a light touch; one of my students described anything beyond a high-five (which she can see coming) or a hug (when she asks for it) as "the devil's touch." Another student who experiences discomfort from fabrics and tags described a popular store as "the place I go to try on really uncomfortable clothes!" Almost half of people with autism are overwhelmed by large crowds, which could be because of any number of their senses being affected, compared with children with ADHD (8%) and typical children (2%) (Mayes et al., 2012). To everyone else, the sensation isn't noteworthy. To the autistic child, it might be torture. Hyperstimulation can lead to sensory overload (Remington & Fairnie, 2017; Sinha et al., 2014), rigidity, or avoidance of the sensations that are so upsetting to them.

Hyposensitivity, or under-responsiveness, has the opposite effect. One time, my mother came home to a trail of wet toe prints down the hallway. If you knew my mother, you'd know she is impeccably clean. Upon investigation, she realized that Danny had walked right through his shoes so that his toes were Fred Flintstone-ing it on the pavement—in winter, no less! He wasn't aware because he couldn't feel it. Now my clever mother always ensures he has back-up shoes. Danny is one of the almost 40% of autistic individuals who have high pain

Textures and tags can cause distress.

tolerance (Mayes et al., 2012) and might not feel the seriousness of an injury (Attwood, 2007) or even realize that this is unusual.

It's important to note that autistic people might be both hyper- and hyposensitive to different inputs. Some folks may seek sensory input and seem to enjoy it, like Danny, who rocks when he talks about his favorite video games. Many of my students toe-walk or flap, especially when enjoying themselves, but sometimes to self-calm. I've also had students with synaesthesia, a condition whereby multiple senses are experienced at the same time, but not all are related to the sensory information provided: one student felt physically sick when he heard certain words; another heard music when he saw colors. Either way, how students with autism process the information around them can be vastly different from their peers.

And they really, really can't handle yelling.

Dealing with Big Feelings

One time, Sonia and I had to talk down our six students after they got off the morning minibus. Talk radio had been blaring news about an epidemic. "What if we get Ebola?" one exclaimed. "My mother's sick. Is she going to die?" "I'm not feeling well!"

We go through this at least once a year. Potential nuclear war with _____ (insert whatever country is currently the focus of media attention). Global warming. Coronavirus. Sometimes there are tears. There are always saucer eyes and *what-if*s.

I asked the bus driver to listen to music stations instead, if possible. It's hard enough for us, as adults, to handle sensationalism in the media, but our students with autism really don't understand that newspapers sell more when they publish bad news than they do with good news. It's in the news so, to them, it must not only be real, it also is an imminent threat. We can help them to perspective-take and use their logical thinking skills to try to counter their anxiety. As if autistic kids don't have enough to be anxious about!

Even when we remove the media, kids with autism experience greater baseline anxiety when compared to peers. When they encounter stressful and new situations, their cortisol levels elevate and stay elevated for longer, even after the event has passed (Spratt et al., 2012). Another study (Wilbarger et al., 2009) showed positive and negative pictures to groups of teens and adults with and without autism. The positive images were things like nature scenes and happy faces while the negative images were things like spiders, car crashes, or people in distress. Both groups had a startle response to the negative images. Only the people with autism had startle responses to positive images, too (Wilbarger et al., 2009). Maybe it was because they couldn't predict what was coming. Whatever the reason, our autistic students are much more stressed than their peers.

It's hard to measure rates of anxiety, because children with autism can't always articulate their feelings and so may under-report, while parents may over-report (see review, MacLennan et al., 2020). In one study, 40% of autistic children were found to have significant anxiety, while 36% met the criteria for clinical depression (Cai et al., 2018). In another, children with high-functioning autism had anxiety (79%), depressed mood (54%), and irritability (88%), as reported by their mothers (Mayes et al., 2011). Children on the spectrum experience symptoms of anxiety more frequently than children with other anxiety disorders, which may be linked to their hyper-reactive responses and the subsequent tendency to later avoid sensory triggers (see review, MacLennan et al., 2020). Their brains react differently to mildly aversive sensory stimuli, lighting up not only the sensory areas of the brain but also their amygdala (fight-flight-or-freeze area), hippocampus (which remembers threats and their contexts), and other areas related to emotional regulation (Green et al., 2013). Interestingly, children with autism might not distinguish real danger, which could be related to their difficulty in reading social situations (Turner & Romanczyk, 2012) or because they are already experiencing maximum anxiety and so their brains don't display a measurable change in activity (Top et al., 2016).

Intense fears or phobias occur in up to 64% of children with autism, including fear of things like punishment, crowds, thunderstorms, or the dark, especially in children with high-functioning autism (see review, Turner & Romanczyk, 2012). More than half of the 1033 autistic children studied by Mayes and colleagues (2013a) had intense fears and phobias, while 41% had what they characterized as unusual phobias to stimuli outside of the norm, including things like toilets, weather, and being sucked up by the vacuum. These unusual fears were more common in girls than boys, though high in both groups. They were sometimes irrational and did not have any relation to age, intelligence, perceived autism severity, or other factors. A dear colleague of mine taught a student who was terrified of wind and who would not go out for recess. To support her, my friend first bought her a thick scarf and helped her wrap it around her face and ears before she went outside. A reward was offered for going outside for short periods of time when there was wind, with the interval gradually building until the fear was no longer so debilitating. I once had a student articulate that, any time he walked into a building, he worried the walls would collapse in on him. Some of these fears are beyond us, as teachers, to remedy and might require support from a multidisciplinary team.

High anxiety—what my student feels on the inside when they have to speak in front of others.

Students can feel overwhelmed during high-pressure situations like tests, even if it is not visible to the teacher.

Dealing with Big Feelings 83

I'm sure you can think of some of the reactions your students have had to anxiety. Sometimes, anxiety is hard to spot because your students with autism don't necessarily show their reactions the way others have learned to do (Uljarević et al., 2016). Some of my students have flat affect, so you can't determine their feelings from their facial expressions. You might be able to tell from their behaviors. In children with autism, this can include the whole range of behaviors, from procrastinating, failing to self-advocate, and being grumpy, to fighting, fleeing, or freezing (Wilbarger et al., 2009). Autistic children—along with other children with executive function deficits—can present as immature or over-reactive (Barkley, 2016). Anxiety increases rigidity, and could lead to difficulties with change, obsessions with topics or routines, or an inability to respond to verbal cues (Mayes et al., 2012). I've seen students get so stuck on a thought that moving on with the day and the group plan was tough. Sometimes this was a vivid memory of a past negative experience or something someone said. One of my students turned into the Hulk four hours after a classroom aide mentioned they owned a German Shepherd. "YOU. DON'T. LIKE. LITTLE. DOGS!" the student exploded, thinking of the fact that he himself owned a Chihuahua. No, the aide insisted, she liked all dogs and just happened to have a big dog. Instead of clarifying at the time, he had dwelled on his misconception all day.

Moving from Co-regulation to Self-regulation

Children with autism often aren't aware of their emotions building and may need prompting to take a break. I once taught a young man who would say he had "anger management" issues. To him, this was a fixed part of his identity. He did not see himself as having any other options. Sonia and I worked hard to teach him a repertoire of strategies at times when things were calm and to prompt them later when things weren't so calm! There were a few explosions in our first month, but each time we neutrally prompted a strategy, like using our calming castle and taking deep breaths, and then gave space. Directives would become less verbal and more gestural. We would not give attention or ask why he was upset until he was calm, and then we would give our full attention. We would react with interest and deep concern only once he was ready to talk and problem-solve, mindful to focus on what to do next time, to avoid shaming for what hadn't gone well, and to praise him for participating in problem-solving and making a good choice by using strategies to calm down. The anger episodes stopped and, as we sent strategies home and asked parents not to intervene during a meltdown with a preferred treat or back massage but to encourage him to independently calm down, he learned he had more control than he thought. He no longer saw himself as "an angry guy."

Students with autism might not always have the words for strong feelings. When talking about emotionally charged events, they might give a bare-bones response or none at all; they may attend less to emotions and mental states of others than their classmates; and they don't show the same pupil response when sentences or words are emotional (see review, Lartseva et al., 2015). One of my students invents her own words for her emotional states—"conblaberated" is a mixture of confusion and happiness! Another student related that he experiences emotions only in extremes. He's angry, anxious, upset, or depressive and bored. He does not recognize himself as having a state of contentment, though this may be due to *alexithymia*, a condition affecting roughly half of all people with autism that makes it difficult for them to identify their feelings (see review, Lartseva et al., 2015). I've seen this student smiling during positive interactions with peers, though he struggles to identify kindness or things he is thankful for when asked during lesson activities. He isn't registering these positive experiences the way he does the negative.

Many of my students arrive in my program having already internalized a sense of difference or being "less than" their peers before they've even learned about their diagnosis. They are fearful of trying something that might be hard for them and might attribute this to their being "stupid" rather than seeing it as a normal part of the learning process for anyone. (I like to tell them that no baby is born being able to walk!) I work very hard to combat this by normalizing different brain strengths and developing areas, featuring Autism Heroes of the day and showing videos of autistic folks talking about their experiences of autism. For most students in my class, a diagnosis is a relief and explains why everything seemed to be so hard for them and they couldn't figure out why. Research also shows children with high-functioning autism have significantly lower self-esteem than other autistic children or typical peers (Mayes et al., 2011). People with autism also tend to feel shame ("I am a bad person") rather than guilt ("I made a mistake") (Davidson et al., 2017), which may explain their reluctance to take any kind of social or academic risk. How hard would it be to make any decision if the outcome regularly tarnished your self-concept?

Student Story: How Autism Can Feel

The thing I struggle with most is anxiety. You start to feel like something terrible is about to happen, and everything just goes black. Every move someone makes is letting the anxiety grow like a weed in your head. It's hard to breathe sometimes as well. People don't always get what is wrong and just leave you alone to calm down by yourself. Sooner or later, you do.

Having autism isn't rare but it can make people feel different from others, or not the same as other people. It's an amazing thing though, because your brain can see things no one else can.

— Grade 5 student

Remember, anxiety is the nemesis of learning! I don't need to convince you that all students can benefit from instruction in managing strong feelings. For students with autism, it is essential. The more aware we are of their emotional states, the more effectively we can support them in recognizing and problem-solving for how to react when they aren't feeling great. We can help them shift from being managed to managing on their own. This might seem daunting, on top of everything else you're expected to do. Take a breath and think about all the ways you are already supporting emotional well-being in your own classroom practice. Teachers do this by nature, in how we structure the environment and in what and how we teach.

Dealing with Big Feelings   85

Structuring the Classroom Environment

Physical Layout

Our class calming castle

Each book you read as a class is an opportunity to promote deeper thinking about thoughts, feelings, perspectives, choices, reactions, and how we relate to characters.

- **Establish a quiet spot.** This could be a couch, a bean bag, or a calming castle students can sit on or in if they need a break without having to leave the room. Teach them your expectations for use: How many minutes? Do they need to ask first? Can they access it at any time, or only during free time and work periods? Decide what works for you.
- **Create alternative workspaces.** Designate a table where students can work if they need a change of scenery. You might wish to indicate that this is the spot students should go to if they need help.
- **Use intentional seating.** Students with attentional issues often do better when closer to the front. This allows you to monitor and to use verbal reminders and proximity to alert them when they need to respond. Pay attention to who distracts whom and whether a student does better in groups or in rows.
- **Stock your classroom with meaningful literature.** Represent diverse ways of thinking and experiencing the world.
- **Use a visual schedule.** Present subjects in order and using a visual to help with instant recognition. A chart that is easy to rearrange and on which you can indicate changes helps students anticipate transitions and feel more at ease.

Sensory Accommodations

Our classroom also has a place where students can find coloring sheets and a variety of mindful exercise cards to use if they need.

- **Declutter the front of the classroom.** Reduce visual distractions, including the visuals on the wall. Think how distracting those neon posters and clashing fonts can be for students with attentional differences.
- **Reduce noise,** especially during assessments and work periods.
- **Explain your expectations for work periods.** Are they allowed to talk? Can they stand to work at their desk? Is it okay if they move to the ground and work there? I usually say that, if students are on task and not disturbing others, I'm flexible how they produce work.
- **Incorporate music.** Play quiet music in the background or use it to encourage transitions. Consider allowing students to listen to music on headphones, which can aid attention.
- **Have free access to fidgets,** but teach the difference between a tool (quiet, stays in your hand, allows eyes to be focused on the board or the person presenting) and a toy (thrown, distracting to others, diverts focus). At first, all students will want to try them, but the novelty wears off. Eventually only those who need them will use them regularly. You can get squeezable items of different weights and textures at any dollar store.
- **Fit chair legs with tennis ball covers.** Collect used tennis balls and cut a cross in them so that they can be fitted over classroom chair legs to reduce noise.
- **Use creative sensory solutions.** Velcro can be stuck to the inside of a desk so that a student with busy hands can run their fingers over it for sensory input.
- **Work in breaks for students who need it.** This can be a pre-arranged deal, such as taking three minutes between a lesson and a work period to sit in the quiet area; or it can be a flexible arrangement by which you assign a portion of work and then tell students they can take a few minutes to color or daydream before getting back on task. Encourage students to ask for a break when they need one. I tell autistic students that others use going for a drink or to the

washroom as natural breaks, so long as they don't ask too often. If they ask too often, you will have to be more specific with your parameters. How many breaks are appropriate in the morning or afternoon? What is an acceptable amount of time and what is allowed?

- **Incorporate movement breaks.** This can be a whole-class approach, or you can encourage stretching any time at the back of the class. You might need to send children with an abundance of energy on errands to give notes or materials to other teachers or to the office.
- **Indicate the expected volume level with a visual.** You can create a volume meter or a levelled chart indicating sound levels, such as Silent/Presenter Voice Only/Quiet Chat/Groupwork Voices/Recess. Practice levels as a class.
- **Dim lights** when watching a video or presentation. You might also want to dim lights at other times, as many autistic folks report being distracted by the frequent flickering cycles of fluorescent lighting that others do not notice.
- **Turn on closed captioning** when watching videos.
- **Decide on routines that make transitions easier**, such as dismissing one row or group at a time to get their snacks or lunch, or to line up at recess.
- **Signal transitions between subjects or tasks using gentle sound**. Get student attention using a rain stick or singing bowl, or by using a quiet call and response, such as, "If you hear me, touch your knees." "If you hear me, touch your shoulders." until everyone is listening.

Classroom Culture

- **Start your day with down time.** If possible, ease students into the day so they can let go of any anxieties from home. This could be ten minutes of silent reading, drawing, building with play clay, coloring, or a guided meditation. I also like to use music and mindfulness after the lunch hour to reset our energy level for the afternoon.
- **Frame mistakes as learning opportunities.** Talk about your own learning process and moments that felt like mistakes. Encourage high-fives when a science experiment doesn't go as predicted (within reason). Do as many growth mindset activities as possible.
- **Teach equity versus equality.** Just as everyone in the room has different strengths and developing areas, they also are working on different things and benefit from different tools. This is why the sensory bin is more effective for some students than others. You can offer different tools to different children based on what they need.
- **Emphasize feedback as part of the process.** It can be tough for kids with autism to handle feedback. They often have low resilience, as when Danny enthusiastically wrote his first (and last) game review online, only to have someone vehemently disagree with him. Teaching that feedback is expected before a work product is considered finished will help students practice and develop grit for the future. Students can practice giving feedback on written work or presentations. You can structure this with visual organizers, such as Two Stars and a Wish, or simply provide guidelines, like "give a compliment and make a suggestion for next time."
- **Encourage trying something new, even for a few minutes.** My team of colleagues and I took 40 kids with autism to an overnight camp for three days. The activities included ziplining, a high ropes course, and a climbing wall. We celebrated every success, whether a child made it all the way through the

activity or simply stepped up one more rung on the ladder. We took photographs so they would have these memories as reference points for next time they were facing a new challenge.
- **Normalize different approaches.** Instil the belief that there's more than one way to do something. Tell students when a question has more than one acceptable answer and encourage taking the risk to venture an answer. Point out it's okay when others have another opinion.
- **Use classroom community circles to problem-solve and to check in how everyone is feeling.** This can happen as needed or at a scheduled time each week. If you have a chatty class, you could pass around a special object that allows the speaker to hold the floor.

Strategies for Emotional Regulation

Talk Accurately about Emotions

I can't emphasize this enough. We want children to realize what is in their power to change. I've had students who embody learned helplessness after years of everyone doing things for them. I've also had students who are confused about their impact and, given their age, no one thinks to tell them. We often assume they know more than they do.

> In the next chapter, we talk about how to handle challenging behaviors. The tips here are to help you navigate how to talk about and teach emotional regulation when children are calm and ready to learn. These are preventative tools rather than crisis management!

Who Is Responsible?

Sonia and some students were walking by the school bulletin board shown here.

The mirrors caught Jeremy's eye on the way to gym class. He turned to Sonia and said, "Wait. I'm responsible for all those things?"

"Yes, you are."

"What about my mom?"

"Yes, she is too."

"Really? Because she says I make her yell."

Sonia saw this as an opportunity to build perspective. "What your mom means is that something you're doing is making her feel frustrated. She is responsible for how she handles that feeling, just like you're responsible for how you react to your feelings. Some people choose to yell. But there are other choices, like we teach you here."

"Oh!"

88   *Connecting Sensory, Anxiety, and Emotional Regulation*

- **Remember, all emotions are valid.** Teach children that big feelings are normal and okay to have. Don't dismiss them for feeling a certain way. Instead, tell them what matters is what we do with our feelings once we have them.
- **Talk about your own feelings.** Sometimes, my students are surprised to learn that I also feel anxious, sad, or angry at times. To them, I am usually so calm and measured, it seems easy. I explain that I've just become better at handling situations with age and practice. Talk about times you've felt big emotions and how you reacted. If you didn't handle it well, talk about what you would do differently.
- **Use literature to discuss the power of feelings and our resulting choices.** We can learn how to deal with feelings through stories and beloved characters!
- **Frame scary current events in a positive way.** In any crisis, I think of Mr. Rogers and how he learned from his mother to look for the helpers. When schools and services shut down because of COVID-19, I suggested to parents they emphasize how communities come together to support the most vulnerable and to help our medical professionals manage the flow of patients needing treatment. It's a way of thinking of others. This is a more helpful way of looking at a difficult situation than hoarding toilet paper!
- **Adopt a problem-solving mindset.** When a child has a problem, empathize but don't perseverate on negative feelings. Instead, shift their thinking to how to handle it. What is it that they want? What might they do or say? Will that have a positive outcome? Talk them through the process, letting them do as much of the thinking as possible. Praise them for being problem-solvers, too!
- **Help students recall past positive events.** My students write in a success book every session and share something they are proud of. I've taught them the distinction between something they're excited about, like a new toy, and something they have earned, worked hard on, tried for the first time, or accomplished, or a way they've helped someone else.
- **Design your own recess check-in.** My friend Jasmine created a beautiful system for her whole class, primarily as a tool to monitor the social experience of our students with autism. She asked everyone in the class to indicate how their recess went with a thumbs-up, thumbs-down, or thumbs-in-the-middle. This enabled her to see anyone who might need more support and showed students how much she cares. She uses it now with every class. Some of her classes have added high-fives or fist bumps to the routine!

Teach New Strategies

For a step-by-step guide, I love Shelley Murphy's *Fostering Mindfulness*.

- **Decide on a timeline and add calming strategies into your routine.** Maybe you want to teach one strategy a week. Maybe you want to have a mindful moment each day. Use this time to practice a wide range of calming activities that could include breathing exercises, guided meditations, gratitude, group laughing, visualization strategies, stretching, mindful coloring, use of a new fidget, or self-affirmations. Pinterest or a quick Google search can help you find these strategies aplenty!
- **Elicit student input.** Create an anchor chart of strategies students suggest! I divide strategies into three categories: physical activities that get out energy, calming activities that slow us down, and thoughts we can think to help us flip our thinking.
- **Imagine safe places.** Lead students through a guided meditation about creating their own imaginary safe place. Give them the freedom to imagine where it

Strategies for Emotional Regulation 89

I got the idea for this from a book called *Moody Cow Meditates* by Kerry Lee MacLean.

is, how it is decorated or furnished, whether it contains animals or people, and what they can do in this space. After, have students draw their safe place.

- **Create a class set of mind jars.** Collect small plastic bottles or sealable spice jars. Add water, a small squirt of dish soap, sparkles, glycerine (to slow down the sparkle movement), and any other sequins or gems students might enjoy watching. After reading the book, we practice watching the sparkles settle along with our minds and then I have each student make their own.
- **Teach replacement thoughts.** Our thinking is what causes the emotions, which cause our reactions. I cut out strips of negative thoughts, like *I am so stupid at math.* or *No one likes me.* and ask students to practice articulating more helpful thoughts, such as *I can ask for help or practice.* or *Not everyone will always like me, but Sarah and Ashleigh ARE my friends.*
- **Be their coach.** Prompt them to use a strategy when you first see the warning signs of a bigger emotion. I once saw Sonia masterfully redirect a possible meltdown by using a soothing voice and saying to a student, "I'm so proud to see you breathing! You are being so mature, calming down so that we can talk about it." The student did not want to disappoint her and so did exactly what she suggested he was doing. Crisis averted!

Model Self-Care

- **Model what to do with big feelings.** What you emphasize, they'll emphasize. How you react, they'll react. Children first learn to manage emotions by watching/interacting with adults, so we should show them that we also use strategies. Tell students when you need a break!
- **Let them help you.** I have asked for students' help when I felt under the weather. They responded with increased patience, better listening, and overall kindness. Another time, before my doctoral thesis defence, I shared with students that I was feeling a bit nervous (so that they would know big feelings happen to everyone). One student told me to drink herbal tea. I spent the weekend steeping and sipping and remembered to let her know the next week. Reinforce empathy by thanking students when they show it and talking about their positive impact.
- **Take care of yourself.** Go to the gym. Take a bath. Cuddle a pet. Call a friend. Do what you need to when you get home to let go of a bad day. One year, I developed a mantra—A.R.R.G.H!! It stands for Accept (the situation you are dealing with), Reflect (no knee-jerk reactions), and Respond (after you've calmed down and had time to think of a thoughtful and gracious response), all of which leads to Good Health!

7

Connecting the *Why* to Behaviors

Emotions are contagious—especially the intense ones. So are reactions. A student digs in their heels and our "Oh, yeah?" instinct begins to kick in, too. A student begins to yell and we feel the need to yell over them. The problem is that these responses don't address the actual reason for the behavior. They can make a conflict grow and do little to prevent future conflicts. If you had a boss who treated you that way, would you ever respect them or be eager to work for them again?

No one will get it right all of the time. Don't beat yourself up for the times you have not lived up to saintly standards of patience. Instead, be reflective about these moments. What would have helped you and your student to de-escalate? What choices might have prevented a power struggle?

Thinking Productively about Behaviors

> I often think of a see-saw when I envision the dynamic between teachers and students with autism during a tense moment. Our reaction can either launch them into a complete meltdown or total withdrawal, or it can bring them gently down.

Reconceptualizing how you think about challenging behaviors can help you respond productively rather than reactively. First, realize that when we label things as *bad behavior* or say, "the apple doesn't fall far from the tree," we are rendering ourselves powerless. The problem is out of our hands. Not only does it not feel good to us, as the adult in the situation, it also presents another problem—we aren't giving children the chance to receive the support they need (Center on the Developing Child, 2011). Dr. Ross Greene (2008) reframes behaviors as a sign that what we are asking a child to do, at that moment, is too difficult for them. No child enjoys being in trouble. If they could do it successfully, they would. What is getting in the way? Instead of assuming it's a motivation issue, recognize it as a lagging-skills issue. On a neurological level, children might not have the essential brain wiring they need to comply with what is being asked. It frustrates them, it frustrates us, and it doesn't help them to build the brain circuitry they need

This is all hard to remember in the midst of a crisis, but gets easier with practice. While being proactive is your first line of defence, here are some helpful strategies for defusing challenging moments that I've learned the hard way!

(National Scientific Council on the Developing Child, 2007). What is so empowering about Greene's method is that we can teach to build skills.

Another psychologist who helped me to see behaviors differently is Dr. Jed Baker (2008). He emphasizes that, as adults, we must expect challenging behaviors will happen, so we can be prepared; we shouldn't take it personally but rather reflect on whether there is anything we're doing that needs to be changed; and we should know that all behaviors are temporary and can be changed with some effort on our part. Someone once told me to think of them as challenging moments, because moments pass. It's changed my mindset!

Words to Say

Remember to use a soothing, quiet tone. If the child is only beginning to show frustration, you can ask them questions and provide choices. If their frustration increases, you will need to tell them what choices you want them to make.

"How can I help you right now?"

"Do you need a break?"

"I see that you're angry. Use a strategy and we'll talk when you're calm."

"Would you like the mind jar or a squeeze ball?"

"Why don't you go for a drink and use the walk back to calm down? Then we'll talk."

"We both need a break before we can solve this. Let's take a moment."

"I'd like you to use the calming castle."

"I want to hear you, but that's hard when you're upset. I'm ready to listen once you're able to talk."

"I'll give you space to think for a moment before we talk about it."

"Let me know when you're ready."

When to Stop Talking

Children with autism lose the ability to process language when upset. It's just like when we're at our breaking point and it's hard to think logically or make good choices. Disengage at these points:

- When it's not helping.
- When the child is becoming more upset.
- When you're becoming more upset.
- When the child cannot follow verbal instructions.

Crisis Management

Consider whether there are times the student is managing. Why are they more successful at those times? We often focus on what isn't working when what is working can tell us a lot!

What NOT to Do	What to Try Instead
Do not insist on task demands at this moment.	Reassure: "It's okay, we can take a break." Reduce demands when they are stressed out. Get to know their body language so you know when they are too challenged by what you are asking. Once they are calm, you can revise the plan or negotiate.
Do not be dismissive of their feelings.	Validate their feelings: "I can see you're feeling upset right now. I want to help you."
Do not threaten.	Instead, redirect to what you would like them to do to calm down.
Do not use body language or expressions that appear threatening.	Keep your face sympathetic. Avoid standing too close or towering over them, which can be scary. If behavior worsens with eye contact, tell them you will give them space. Stop looking at them but keep them in your line of sight.
Do not yell.	Use a quiet, soothing voice, or stop speaking altogether. (The exception is when a student is about to make an unsafe choice, like running into traffic or hitting another child. I can count on one hand the number of times I've had to yell. Both times, it was in response to a safety hazard and my raised voice stopped the child in their tracks. They were not habituated to it, so it was an effective tool. I immediately dropped my voice to thank them for stopping and encouraged them to walk away, take a break, etc.)
Do not continue to repeat instructions if the child has not shifted their behavior after you've made several verbal attempts.	Give processing time between directives. If this doesn't work, cease talking. You can gesture to indicate what you would like them to do or give them space so they can become less overstimulated.
Do not grab them, especially without proper restraint training or another adult present.	If they are exhibiting unsafe behavior, you might wish to evacuate the classroom and send for help. Remove scissors or other potential harmful objects from their reach. Keep your distance. Remember, property can be replaced. In the last decade, I've evacuated the classroom only once. It was in my first year before I knew how to be proactive and disengage when needed.

Do not ask others to join in the power struggle.	It is okay to invite another adult in to be another set of eyes, but only one person should engage with the child at a time or the student will be more easily overwhelmed by the increased processing demands. If the child is reacting badly to you, it may be wise to trade off with someone else, especially if they know them better. Also tell students, "We give space to classmates when they are upset." Tell them not to make eye contact or to talk to the student until they are calm.
Do not ask them to problem-solve too early.	Sometimes you must leave problem-solving for another time. If a child begins to get upset again as you talk, let them know it's okay to take time to calm down before you can both come up with a plan. Inform their parents what happened and what you hope will happen next time so that they can support and reinforce your message at home. Talk the next day.

For incredibly challenging behaviors, it is important to reach out to other professionals who can help assess the function of the behavior and put in place a plan that everyone connected with the child can reinforce. That said, autistic students who can express themselves are often the best resource.

Discovering the *Why?*

I highly recommend checking out Dr. Ross Greene's books and website (www.livesinthebalance. org) where he models his "collaborative and proactive solutions" three-step Plan B approach to problem-solving with a child, which involves empathizing, sharing perspectives, and agreeing on a solution to try.

See page 105 for a Problem-Solving template; page 106 for the When I'm Upset I Can… template for preventative strategies.

Your next task is to sit down with your student and talk it out. What happened? What were they thinking and feeling at the time? Listen more than you speak. Your goal is to identify what the problem was, from their perspective. Be flexible with how you expect them to respond. Several students have been more expressive when given the option to write or type their answers to my questions. Hearing from them directly is the key and prevents your jumping to a conclusion about why they were upset. You will often be surprised by what they were actually thinking and feeling. Once you know the *why*, you can figure out what skills you need to teach them (Greene, 2008).

Let's imagine a student pushes someone during snack time. After a challenging moment, the best question I have learned to ask is "When you did that, what was it you wanted to happen?" (Asking why they did something will usually increase defensiveness and gets you nowhere.) Instead, you might find out they wanted space and didn't know how to ask for it, or maybe the other child was teasing them and they didn't know how to handle it. Once you know what they wanted, you can ask them if there would be a better way to get it next time. Whatever the problem was, share what you feel were choices that made the problem grow and that you don't want to see in the future. Ask them what they could do differently next time so that no one would feel unsafe or upset, or end up in trouble. Maybe they needed to take a break and then to ask for help. Maybe there was room to negotiate task demands at the time. Come up with ideas together.

Sometimes, if the child is having difficulty perspective-taking when problem-solving, you might want to draw the situation. Usually, Sonia or I draw the stick figures. We then add in thought and speech bubbles, encouraging the child to express what the other people involved might be thinking or feeling. Then we have them draw what to do next time or record a list of strategies to use. You can then share drawings and strategies with parents and teachers to use as a visual aid with the child in other settings.

Deciding the *Now What?*

Now, what about consequences? When we use the lagging-skills framework, we understand behavior happens as a result of our demands on a child who isn't ready to meet them in that moment. Maybe they're overstimulated by the environment. Maybe they didn't sleep well. Maybe anxieties and frustrations have built up so that something they would normally be able to do just wasn't possible the moment we expected it. These aren't excuses, but rather mitigating factors that will affect how well our student can cope and make good choices.

> Consequences should never happen in isolation. The word *discipline* comes from the Latin word for "learner." If they're not learning, it's not effective discipline. Our end goal is to help our students (and us!) learn how to handle things more productively in the future. Keep that goal in mind when deciding the *now what?*

What Doesn't Work

- **Suspensions.** Full suspensions never work for kids with autism, unless it's a kid for whom school is the ultimate reward. A kid who is suspended and goes home to where there are no task demands and they have access to games, preferred items, and comfy spaces is not going to learn that what they did resulted in something bad. You may see an increase in behaviors, because what did they learn? Yelling and throwing a stapler got them a break. This tells us two things. They clearly needed a break to begin with. It also tells us that, for serious behaviors, an in-school suspension might be preferable (Barkley, 2016). A quiet setting, still with task demands but without access to highly preferred items like technology, will be a more effective consequence.
- **Shaming.** Remember how people with autism feel shame (a negative feeling about themselves) when they do a bad thing? You want to keep your conversation geared toward how they can learn and improve for next time. You want them to feel safe to let you know what is bothering them before a challenging moment occurs. You want this to build your relationship, not damage it further.
- **Angry tone and raised volume.** Remember, how we say something influences whether it is heard. Angry tone and volume inspire fear and damage trust, and if you find yourself using one, I'd bet it doesn't make you feel good either. It also tends to be a trap you fall into and can't get out of. Adults keep yelling, but the behavior doesn't change.
- **Unpredictable punishments and fear tactics.** Punishments that are severe and without a clear connection to the behavior, like taking away recess for a whole week because they wouldn't come to the carpet, won't be effective. The child won't see the link between what they did and what the result is. They will just perceive the person wielding the power as an unfair tyrant! This isn't to say there shouldn't be consequences, but they must be logical. The punishment must fit the crime, so to speak.

Types of Consequences that Work

Being expected to problem-solve and make an agreement is a natural consequence. So is repairing the situation, if appropriate. While not part of Greene's method, I've found it helps children with autism to recognize their impact if you

Deciding the Now What? 95

ask them to consider whether they need to socially repair a situation. If they used words that upset a friend or frightened someone, they may wish to apologize verbally or in a text. An apology usually includes exactly what you brainstorm together: what isn't going to happen again or what they plan to do differently next time. You might choose to mediate a conversation between students. I once had a student who *needed* to speak to his whole class to explain his reaction so that he could feel comfortable again. He was worried about what they would think of him, and so prepared a short speech and read it to the class. They knew him well and it had his desired effect. This was his choice, and not something I'd recommend foisting on any child!

Social repair could also take the form of tidying up a mess if they made one. If they start, it can be a gesture of kindness for you to join them in this task. I often find, in the aftermath of a challenging moment, the student feels badly about themself. You want to express, in words and actions, that you still care about them. This is a learning moment to help you both determine how to handle a similar situation in the future.

Another natural consequence is informing families. I let students know that, while I'll always inform a parent about a serious challenging moment, if the student participated in problem-solving, I'm also going to say how proud I was that they were able to do that. When I call or email parents about a challenging moment, I encourage them to have calm conversations at home that support the skills being taught. If we know what situation upsets the child, a parent can prepare them, reminding them of the strategies to try. Any consequence for a behavior in my setting should take place in my setting, or be presented as a joint approach between home and school in a meeting where everyone comes together with the child.

New routines and increased surveillance are usually an inevitable consequence. Imagine a student has been sneaking YouTube videos instead of using their school device to work. Together you problem-solve, make a plan, and lay out the expectations of when they can and can't watch YouTube. As you have a student practice and develop a new habit, they will probably feel they are being watched like a hawk and prompted by the teacher. They may not like it and that's okay. They will most definitely test to see if you mean what you say. Increased monitoring is effective because you can redirect immediately and send a clear message of your expectations. They might express discontent. That's fine. I explain to them calmly that, when rules are followed, it shows me students are responsible and able to handle the trust given. If they can't, we develop a plan and they need to show that they can handle the situation over time before I or another adult monitoring the situation can step away. I believe they can do it, but I have to help them get there.

Pro tip: I encourage parents to use similar systems and logical consequences at home too, such as explaining,

> "It's expected that you finish work first before video games. When you follow these rules, it shows me how mature you are, and I want to give you more time to do what you like. When you don't follow the rules, it shows me you're not ready yet to manage your time on your own, and it means I have to keep the device."

The behavior and the consequences are very clearly connected and you reference the cause and effect together.

On rare occasions, a more significant consequence will be needed. Serious behaviors necessitate a serious response, because the reality is that if as an adult they show physical aggression or unsafe behaviors, they could face much more serious real-life consequences. As mentioned, in-school suspensions can be used and should include a meeting with the student and the family to connect the consequence to the behavior. Sometimes the loss of a privilege may be needed.

Pairing Consequences with Teaching

I had one student who displayed significant disruptive and non-compliant behaviors in class and at recess. He knew that we earn reward outings as a group in my program, both through individual goals and through showing expected safety behaviors, so he would be good the week or two before a trip and earn the class trip with his peers. On one outing, he wouldn't cross the road safely and later picked up a rock and threw it at a window. In speaking with his home school, they let me know this wasn't unusual and on a recent field trip with his large class, he lay in the middle of a ski hill, laughing, and refused to move. The school did not implement a consequence because they weren't sure how to proceed. I considered what message that would send: that he could do whatever he wanted, without consequence. No learning new skills.

So I spoke with his parent and let them know that I felt the dangerous behaviors were important to address with the removal of the next trip, but that he could still earn future events. We would spend the time he would have been on the trip emphasizing what to do differently next time and monitoring and building the skills we wanted to see. After missing the trip, he would have to regularly show specific safety behaviors to earn a future outing. We made it clear what our expectations were. Sonia developed a fabulous chart for tracking the target skills each day as a visual reminder of what we wanted to see from him. We discussed the chart multiple times a day. We made some visuals and sent a social script home for daily review. As a graduated step toward full trip independence, we also asked that a family member come on the next earned trip. While we didn't think we'd see the same behaviors, we wanted him to know he was being monitored until we knew he could handle the situation. The trip after that, we asked the family to be available by phone in case we needed their support. He was an angel on all future trips that year, including our overnight trip.

One time, a student lost a trip for extremely aggressive behaviors, such as kicking or punching a specific peer, usually in response to some minor annoying behavior that student exhibited. This would happen so quickly there was no opportunity to redirect or intervene. We used a strategy similar to the one outlined on page 96. The day it happened, there was an immediate loss of privileges. No video games at the end of day (students know from the first day how to earn this privilege and what behaviors would result in its loss). When it happened twice more, the student's parent and school were informed what happened and we decided that he would not be coming on the next week's trip. Instead, we held a meeting. His principal offered to drive the family to my school, and we sat down as a group to discuss the loss of the next trip and our expectations for behavior and stress management going forward. My principal used the school code of conduct as a visual, highlighting the specific infraction and why it wasn't allowed. The student's parent supported at home by having the student work on

Deciding the Now What? 97

an apology note for the other child. The student shared his feelings and developed a visual of six strategies he could use next time he was frustrated; this visual was sent to all settings. We wanted to develop other proactive strategies, so we asked him whether he would appreciate a break when he arrived after a long bus drive with the other child. He began going to the gym for five minutes with Sonia to shoot some hoops. And something magical happened: he began opening up to her. We reassured him that, if he ever needed our help, we would intervene—but we would need more than a millisecond to process. We worked on a cueing system so that we could know when he was upset. We let him know this would allow us not just to work on his feelings, but also to give our attention to helping the other student understand his own impact. In the end, he saw us as supportive of him, rather than critical. There was no more hyper-reactivity toward the other student, perhaps because he knew we were watching and willing to help, and he remembered to take breaks if he needed. I'd send his mother emails with good news: "He had a great day today! He played and included everyone. There were no issues at all." He knew we were proud of him and we made a big deal about his ability to manage his emotions, especially in interactions with the other child. No exaggeration—it worked so well that they became friends.

The caveat when removing a privilege is to do your best to communicate the potential loss in advance, when it can still be earned. Explain the expectations and let the student and their family know if they are on track or not. If not, what do they need to get back on track? What will you put in place to help them? Removal of a privilege should not be arbitrary. Trips are not usually earned in large class settings, so the removal of a trip as a privilege might be an equity issue. It would warrant a discussion with administration before talking to parents and must be in response to a significant misbehavior. *It is a last resort.* When we plan trips, we should be thinking of trips our autistic students can already manage. There are other possible strategies, like inviting a family member to help support, adding a dedicated staff person to accompany the child, and choosing a highly structured trip that is of limited duration. Showing pictures and reviewing rules and expectations beforehand can minimize unpredictability and anxiety. We don't want to exclude children with autism from social opportunities. We need to balance safety and preparation. We must put in place supports to help them to be successful in the settings where we expect them to perform well.

Strategies for Maximizing Outcomes

Here are some strategies to implement in the aftermath of a challenging moment to help regain a sense of calm and order. There are also proactive tips to keep it that way!

Ongoing Check-ins and Goal-Setting

Not long ago, Sonia and I had to speak to a student for a minor misstep where he got a bit silly in a drama scene and upset his scene partner. When we asked him to speak to us in the hallway, his eyes widened and he said, "Am I in trouble?"

"No, you're never in trouble with us. We need to problem-solve and learn, but you're not in trouble."

One of the nearby students commented, "That's why I love coming here."

As with problem-solving, students may not be used to this approach at first. They may not be forthcoming as you invite them to share their perspectives. What is fascinating is how quickly they adapt. Once you've checked in with them a few times, they realize you want to listen and help.

Sonia and I remind students that every day is a clean slate. We're aiming for the day to be better than our last. If we've problem-solved a challenging moment, that is enough. We continue treating the child with respect and encouragement. We don't react as though we anticipate bad behaviors (even if we do!). We control our faces and keep our voices calm. We consider whether we've reacted in a way that contributed to the situation and make changes if needed. We let the child know we're rooting for them. Because when they're doing well and feeling good, we are too. Remind yourself of that: tomorrow is a new day—for everyone.

We don't use conferencing only when things aren't going as we would like. We conference each week with each student. You might not be able to do this as often or as in-depth as we can, but regular check-ins and talking about what they are working on helps reduce their anxiety and is a way to keep everyone's eye on the prize. It's the same technique you use to problem-solve challenging behaviors; however, instead of one specific problem, you can ask a student about how they're doing in class or at recess, what they feel they've done well recently, and what they want to work on to improve. You can use this with any student in your class.

Try to set one or two goals for the student to focus on. It's great if they can suggest goals but, if they aren't self-aware yet, you can suggest what to work on. Maybe it's greeting a classmate. Maybe it's working on their own for five minutes before asking for help. Decide, discuss, and come up with ideas to try to make the goal(s) achievable for the child each week. You can write down the goal and track it each day to the best of your ability. In the beginning, you can remind a student about a goal before the goal is expected to be needed. Give lots of positive reinforcement when you see them working on a goal. Next time you sit down to check in, review the chart together and discuss whether they tried any of the ideas you collaboratively brainstormed the time before.

Plans can always be revised during check-ins. For example, one of my students loved hugging his teachers. These hugs were happening at any time, all day long. He was like a hug ninja! It was cute when he was in Grade 3 but was becoming less so as he got older. First we worked on asking before hugging, to decrease personal space invasions. Then I asked him to look around at his Grade 6 classmates to see whether they were still hugging the teacher every day. He realized the rules had changed. We reviewed other ways teachers and students show they care for one another, developing our own goodbye ritual. We also set guidelines: You can ask for a hug on special occasions or before a long break. This young man was very clever and began asking for hugs for Kwanzaa, Hanukkah, Christmas, Boxing Day, New Year's, Chinese New Year—you name it! So we regrouped and clarified some new expectations.

Goals not only change as they are mastered, but can also become more detailed and complex as a new skill is learned. If an autistic student is working on greeting a classmate, you can extend the skill by adding a detail (e.g., with a smile) or another component (e.g., facing the classmate, listening to the response, and making a follow-up question or comment). Start small; add on! If the student is struggling with a goal, it can be made more specific or broken down to smaller components so that the child can be more successful in achieving it. If working independently for five minutes each work period is too demanding throughout the entire day, maybe only track their ability to work independently in Language and, as they master that, add Math to the mix. Or you could begin even smaller: the goal starts as "I will read what the question is asking and try to complete the first question on my own," and its demands are gradually increased in manageable chunks. Start from where they are comfortable and gradually increase what is being asked.

Strategies for Maximizing Outcomes 99

Sample goal chart

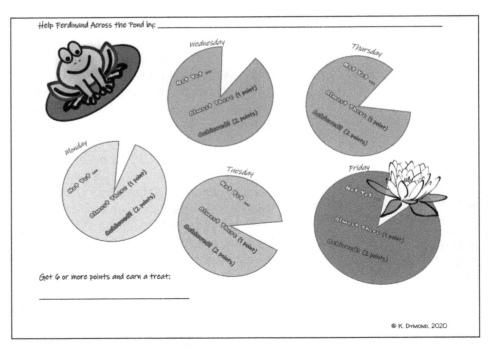

We'll talk about effective reward systems in the next chapter.

As students work on goals, you will want to consider having them earn points toward a prize, activity, free time, or homework pass to keep them motivated. In my program, since everyone is working on goals, we bank points for various group rewards. It's a great way to promote the idea that we support one another. Sometimes children with autism might need a more supportive reward system to work on goals that are harder to master.

You may be thinking how difficult it is to track a goal every day. You can also transition to having the student self-assess their goal(s) and, if they are accurate, consider rewarding them with bonus points or small prizes (Barkley, 2016). Check-ins become easier and shorter because you and the student both have the same goal. The idea is to move gradually from supporting the skill to independent completion.

See page 107 for a Weekly Check-In template.

A bonus of check-ins is that, over time, you put ownership on students to identify what they need or what strategies they can employ to improve. It teaches them what is in their power to improve and how to self-advocate. My students work on self-advocacy projects near the end of their time in the program. I'll never forget watching one student typing:

I want my classmates to know I have problems.

He paused and read to himself. He deleted the period.

I want my classmates to know I have problems communicating with others.
They can help me by starting conversations and spending time with me.

Giving Attention

The toughest students I've had tend to fall into two categories. First are the kids you could consider attention seekers—the ones who don't distinguish between good or bad attention, they just want all eyes on them. They may feel they aren't the smartest or the coolest in the room, so they try to establish an identity that sets them apart. The unfiltered comic. The disruptor. The defender of all students' rights! They seem to take up more space and more time than anyone else.

This is the kid to spend time with. This is the kid you want to get to like you. Make them your assistant. Have them collect the pizza money. Ask them to fix your computer problem. Sit down beside them and watch them drawing or playing a game on their phone. Ask for their advice for a song or video to play to the class (but preview it first). Give them responsibilities, such as class photographer or attendance runner. You can tie these privileges to moments you caught them being good: "I noticed you were helping your desk mate today, and I could also use your help" or "Thanks for all the positive contributions in class today! I need someone to help me set up the projector. Could you help me?"

What I've found is that, when you give a child trust and responsibility, they will usually live up to it. If they don't, you problem-solve and decrease their freedoms temporarily, explaining why you're going back a step. They won't like that. During check-ins, you can also talk to them about what types of comments you're looking for in lessons. Shut down unexpected comments firmly but without much emotion, such as: "I'm looking for realistic answers" or "Try again"; or you can remove all attention by ceasing eye contact and gesturing for them to stop, while picking someone else. When their answers are the types you want, relish them. Become animated! Declare to the class, "I hope everyone heard what Eddie just said! He made a great point..." You want to make them prefer the positive attention. Even if their words and actions are negative, you want to treat them fairly and in a manner the students in your class can emulate. Because your other students will follow your example!

The other type of student that can wear the nerves of even the most experienced of teachers is the attention-averse child. They might resist any instruction. They might snap when you give them feedback, positive or negative (Attwood, 2007). They might refuse to comply with a request. Their anxiety triggers a highly reactive defensive posture with any perceived threat to their ego. Don't let this deter you from giving them feedback. They'll need to learn how to take it, after all. You can start by depersonalizing instructions. You might want to let them know about transitions between subjects by saying, "According to the schedule, it's now time for Math"; "The curriculum we are learning teaches it this way"; or "The principal's rules are..." This way, the instructions are not always coming from you but from an external source. You can also write an instruction or feedback on a sticky note and stealthily drop it off and walk away before they can object. Give them time to process a request before asking them again.

Compliments can also trigger a strong reaction. This usually happens with a child who has low self-esteem and perfectionism. They never feel good enough and severely doubt you mean what you say. They are frustrated with themselves if something is hard or doesn't measure up to their vision. You can test the waters by complimenting the group around them: "I love how everyone is working here!" When giving verbal feedback on a presentation, avoid saying their name; instead, praise the design of the presentation or a specific point of knowledge, and avoid eye contact. Try giving a personal specific compliment in writing or using a visual thumbs-up. I will increase the feedback intensity with time and greater relationship, eventually explaining the feedback rules:

> "I am a teacher. My job is to give feedback to help all students to improve or to let them know when I think they're doing something great. The compliments I give are based on my observations and don't require the student to

Strategies for Maximizing Outcomes 101

agree with it. If the student immediately tries to do something bad to negate my compliment, I tell them we aren't our choices. I notice the good qualities in my students and these stay in my memory. I recognize that they'll still sometimes make choices that don't serve them well as part of their learning. Just because they made one choice that wasn't helpful to them or others, doesn't mean they aren't smart, kind, or valuable to our class. My opinion about who they are as a person is not so easily changed!"

Using Accountability Language

Over the years, I've learned to shift how I ask or assign things to help all students and to avoid power struggles. I call this *accountability language*. First, let me show you what this is NOT:

"This is your last warning.!

"If you don't do what I've asked, you'll get detention!"

"Don't even think about doing that!"

These are options that increase anxiety and damage your relationship, just as would happen if you had an employer who used tactics like these.

You can achieve the same goals by using language that builds in student accountability and teacher trust. Accountability language looks like this:

"This is a reminder that I want you to take out your agenda and write down what's on the board. I'll give you a moment."

"I want everyone to finish this assessment in class so it doesn't need to go home. Make a good choice!"

"I'm excited to read your thoughts. I'll check back in a few minutes."

"I can't wait to see your comic. I'm going to give you some time to get started."

If it repeatedly doesn't work, it's a sign you need to investigate why and whether your expectations are achievable.

These types of responses make it clear what you want them to do. Almost every student will respond with the way you wish if you walk away and give them the time to think about what is being asked. And it works with everyone!

The Power of Rapport

As a student teacher, I had a practicum in a Grade 7 gifted class. I had been warned that Simon was chronically disengaged and handed nothing in. As I taught a creative writing unit, I made sure to circulate. The first session, I noticed he'd only produced a single sentence in a substantial period. My goal was to connect with him. I asked if I could read what he had so far. It was only a sentence, but it truly set a scene and was captivating. I said something like, "What a powerful opening. I can't wait to hear what comes next." Each day, no matter how much he produced, I gave immediate descriptive feedback on what was produced and positively reinforced the progress. I encouraged the next step and gave him room to breathe.

---

102   *Connecting the* Why *to Behaviors*

The way I see it, it's important not to chastise, but to encourage, because kids rise and fall to your expectations. I have never been disappointed when I have given students the respect and the processing time to make the choice to be accountable for their own work. Although I asked for only one story, Simon turned in two in the end. He was a phenomenal writer. I wrote on my assessment form that one of his stories reminded me of Cormac McCarthy's novel *The Road* and I hoped he'd continue developing his gift. When I came back to visit, he'd read the McCarthy book and wanted to talk to me about it. That was one of those moments that served as a reminder of the importance of connecting.

Connecting as a Village
Establishing a Partnership with Families

Supporting kids with autism requires a team approach. Lessons you teach will be better remembered if you and parents are doing similar things, talking about why the goals set are important, and presenting as a partnership. And families really need that from schools. Receiving a diagnosis can be incredibly painful. It requires parents to rethink their expectations and plans for their child. Acceptance is a journey and it can be frustrating, as teachers, to want parents to be further along in the journey than they are ready or able to be. One of the hardest parts of raising a child with any special needs is feeling alone and judged for your every decision. What you may not see is how the whole family has to adapt. Siblings must get used to a little less attention and greater independence. Parents who, from the outside, might look like they're disengaged might be working extra shifts to afford private therapies. They could be burned out from trying to get everything right when there is no one-size-fits-all approach, but only what works for each specific child.

But the very hardest part is the worry. I know this from my own parents and from the many parents I've met over the years. When I was in teachers' college, I worked with an autistic man in his first year of college. His mother told me her son was her entire world and she was driven by the fear of what would happen to him when she's gone. This might be the parent who comes across as demanding the moon without recognizing the limitations of the educational system. So try to keep perspective when communicating with parents. Here are some tips for parent communication:

- **Find what you have in common.** Parents are much more assured and open when they know you want the same things, and that you understand and care for their child. Let them know that together you are a team!
- **Communicate successes as well as areas where growth is needed.** Send emails or notes, or make phone calls. I've had parents tell me that every time the phone used to ring, they feared their child was in trouble again. When I first started emailing or calling, it was the first time anyone had had anything good to say about their child. Find ANYTHING good to say!
- **Don't let the report card be the first time they hear something is not working.** Keep parents apprised of challenges you and their child are having.
- **When raising concerns, use objective language.** Describe the behaviors that are problematic instead of labelling them with a value judgment or a diagnosis they don't have (this is especially helpful when raising concerns about unidentified students).

Dr. Ross Greene has a tool available on his website called the *Assessment of Lagging Skills and Unsolved Problems* that is free to use and can help you to find the right words and identify what needs to be taught.

Strategies for Maximizing Outcomes 103

- **Tell them what you've already tried.** Just like when you talk with students, the goal of the conversation should be to solve a problem and create a plan. Otherwise, talking about challenges can sound like complaining or blame.
- **Ask for their input.** Have they seen this behavior at home? (Often the answer is no, because the demands are different at home and at school.) If they have, how do they address it? Is there a unified approach you can take?
- **State what you plan to try next.** Part of the plan should include when and how you will keep parents informed about how things are going. This could include asking them for help with a reward system or talking to their child about a problem. Ongoing communication is key.
- **Let families know you can always come back to the drawing board.** Just like with students, no plan is final. If something isn't working, it can be readjusted.

Building the Understanding of Colleagues

Our students may work with other teachers and educational staff who don't yet know their weaknesses and strengths. They may be supervised in the yard or at lunch by staff or monitors who don't know them. They may have substitute teachers who are not informed of their needs. Why not reduce the guesswork?

- **Each year, pass on relevant information to next year's teacher.** Tell them what was easy or hard for the student, strategies that worked, and what you found that motivated the student.
- **Ask your principal if you can share about students needing some extra TLC at a staff meeting.** Communicate the student's needs and how staff can best help and form rapport with the student. One of my research participants shared that her school had a system in place whereby everyone on staff was informed of a goal the child was working on. If it was greeting, everyone in the school would try to say hello and wait for a response, informing the teacher of each success. If it was joining in at recess, staff would be extra mindful to prompt interactions.
- **If you feel comfortable, deliver a lunch-and-learn session on autism.**
- **Assign at-risk students a secret advocate on staff.** This staff member can watch out for them, try to build a positive relationship, and work behind-the-scenes to meet their needs. This is even better if it happens to be next year's teacher, so there is already some rapport!
- **Prepare substitute teachers.** Include information in your notes on how to interact with any students with autism. Many of my students have encountered conflicts with substitute teachers for their reactions, lack of filter, and literal thinking. They often had no idea why they were in trouble. Usually the substitute teacher had no idea they had an invisible disability. Create a community where we set up students for success by setting up colleagues for success, too.

Problem-Solving

What Happened		What I Can Do Next Time	
How Others Felt	**How I Felt**	**How Others May Feel**	**How I May Feel**

Name: _____

When I'm Upset I Can...

THINK

CALM DOWN BY ...

GET MY ENERGY OUT BY...

Name: _____

Pembroke Publishers ©2020 *The Autism Lens* by Kara Dymond ISBN 978-1-55138-347-7

Weekly Check-In

Name: _____ Week of _____ Self-Assessment/Teacher Assessment (*circle one*)

My Goal: _____

	Monday	Tuesday	Wednesday	Thursday	Friday
Done Independently					
Done with a Little Support					
Done with a Lot of Support					
Partially Done					
Not Done					
No Chance to Assess					

Notes (*What went well? Was any part of the goal easy? Was any part hard? What could be better next time?*)

Discussion

Strategies to Try (*What to think or do to make it easier; visuals that might help; a gesture or words your teacher can say or make; etc.*)

Goal Adjustments

❑ Keep for now   ❑ Edit/Add: _____   ❑ Mastered! Move on to _____

Pembroke Publishers ©2020 *The Autism Lens* by Kara Dymond ISBN 978-1-55138-347-7

8

Connecting through Strengths and Interests

I like to start where we should always begin: with student strengths and passions.

My students live and breathe their interests. They spend most of their time outside of school, at recess, and even while daydreaming in class thinking about them. And it can pay off! Over the last decade, my classroom has been blessed with terrific artists, mathematicians, cooks, comedians, kids teaching themselves university-level physics in Grade 4, and any other talent you can imagine.

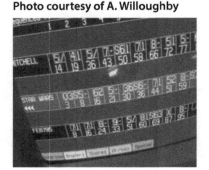

"My screen name reflects my future estimation of my last two frame scores."
Photo courtesy of A. Willoughby

Be Prepared to Be Dazzled

I've been stumped by some of the incredible skills exhibited by kids with autism, like former student Timothy who, when on a school trip, selected his moniker for the bowling screen: FE8795. His teacher asked him what it meant, because everyone else was picking things like their own names (how logical) and Star Wars (their special interest!). Timothy explained, "It's my future estimation of my last two frame scores." His teacher kindly sent me a photo of the score board and his last two frames: How did he do it? Please, let us know if you figure it out!

Outside of school, I've run into autistic individuals like a young man named Phil who came to my church and was turning around in his seat, fascinated by the organ. After mass, I invited him up to the loft. He asked the organist if he knew a particular classical piece of music, and the organist said, "Yes, but I'd need the music to do it justice." Phil plopped himself down on the organ bench and began to play the piece—perfectly! His mother turned to me and said, "He's never even had a piano lesson!" Phil also had an intellectual disability and required significant care to function. As he played, he told me to sing along. It was a moment that will stay with me the rest of my life. It reminded me that, while not every autistic person has a skill that takes your breath away, everyone has something to offer.

The thing to keep in mind about the fascinations of people with autism—especially when we're giving students reminders to put them away and pay attention to the lesson—is that they can be harnessed for different purposes, including building relationships, increasing engagement in lessons, deepening understanding, helping to persevere through harder tasks, gradually expanding interests, boosting self-esteem, and as a bridge to classmates.

Grabbing and Holding Student Interest

Sonia and I try to brush up on the video games, characters, and concepts our students like so we can reference them in our goal-setting. My student Jamie loved all things dinosaurs and was extraordinarily slow lining up for recess. I connected these during conferencing by asking him how he might activate his "raptor speed." He loved this analogy and started telling me how hard it is, when he feels more like an allosaurus! We brainstormed ways velociraptors and allosauruses (allosauri?) are different, to which I could contribute extraordinarily little. We identified how a "recess raptor" might be alerted to the cues it's time to line up. In short, we made problem-solving fun. Sometimes, you get more out of students when you use terms they enjoy.

Just as we tap into prior knowledge before teaching something new, teachers should also think about the wealth of knowledge our students possess and what might resonate most with our harder-to-reach ones. Their interests are like the hub of a wheel, from which everything else can branch. I had a student fascinated by all things mechanical who would poke holes in my wheel comparison if he were reading this! That's okay. You may never understand their fascinations at their level. They're the experts. As Dr. Paula Kluth (2018) says, "You don't have to understand someone's passion in order to honor it."

Although every child in your class will do better when they are fascinated by the topic, engagement is essential to learning for children with autism. Other kids intuitively know to turn their eyes to the front and get through less preferable tasks or lessons. Kids with autism don't, and it is hard to compete with their brilliant imaginations, mental replays of Minecraft and memes, artistic pursuits, or whatever else is occupying their attention instead of the lesson. Especially in their least favorite subjects, finding a hook can be your entry point to materials that would otherwise have them glazing over. Is there a way you can use a strength to enhance learning? Perhaps that budding musician can write a song about a concept, or your graphic novelist can illustrate key parts of the story. Unless you are assessing writing mechanics, is it possible for them to produce knowledge in other ways besides writing?

Using technology is an automatic win, as it seems to grab and hold the attention of autistic students far better than just talking. This is partly because they tend to better process visual information, but also because technology reduces anxiety while increasing socialization and independence (Hedges, Odom, Hume, & Sam, 2018). I've been known to give an instruction in a character's voice, as a humorous way to remind a student to get back on track. We can make spontaneous choices or, even better, plan with students in mind. Think whether you have done any of the following:

- included one of their interests in lessons or activities (e.g., journal prompt, math problems, video)

- incorporated technology into lessons or lesson responses
- varied the types of lesson activities throughout the day so that it is not all pen and paper
- used visuals to bolster comprehension
- made room for choice (e.g., independent project, novel study)
- provided options for lesson tasks (e.g., organizers, levelled readings)
- provided options for final products (e.g., speech, comic, animation, essay)
- provided options for presenting knowledge (e.g., present to me, present to three, or present by pre-recorded video)
- built in opportunities to gauge their interests (e.g., tickets out the door, voting on topics they want to learn about)
- built in opportunities for their strengths to shine

Any one of these choices helps make your classroom even more inviting for students. Also try to find times to welcome their personal connections. After a lesson on how to move from acquaintances to friends to close friends, one of my students related, "I get it! Levelling up a friendship is like evolving a Pokémon; you have to put in more time and effort at each stage!" She has no idea how many of my students since have benefitted from her analogy!

Effective Reward Systems

If a goal of the day or action plans don't seem to cut it, a child might be struggling to complete what is being asked. Sometimes it needs to be broken down more. Sometimes we need to sweeten the deal. Imagine you're suddenly asked to take on a giant task at work requiring overtime and effectively doubling what you need to do, but for no additional pay. It would be hard to complete it wholeheartedly, especially if you weren't sure of the long-term benefits. Just like us, people with autism may be more likely to work on new goals (which are hard for them) when there are incentives.

Incentives are not bribery. As someone once explained to me, bribery is when you give someone something before you ask them to do something. Rewards are given after someone meets your expectations. Children with autism may need reward systems for those harder-to-master skills. Given that they don't always think about cause and effect or long-term benefits, they aren't motivated the same way other students might be. They aren't thinking about the marks, your feelings, or that they may need the skill later. All that matters is how they feel about themselves in that moment. Like anyone, they want to avoid feeling embarrassed or like a failure. So why on earth should they scale the mountain we've placed in front of them? Incentives are a way to acknowledge just how hard the child is working on something, in addition to the curriculum and social dynamics, which are also hard for them. For a reward system to be successful, we need to have already taught them the skills (after all, it would be foolish to try mountaineering without the proper equipment), we have to encourage them on the journey, and the reward (the view from the top) has to be worth it! It can help them to overcome their reluctance to practice new skills.

> If you use a reward system in your classroom, it should include three components: what they will earn, how they will earn it, and how frequently it will be earned.

Possible Rewards

Whatever you decide to offer must work for you and your classroom reality. But whatever reward or choice of rewards you decide on, it has to be motivating for the child (Barkley, 2016). Rewards can sometimes lose their effectiveness, but offering the child a choice of rewards or asking them what they want to earn reduces this risk. You can be creative! Parents can also be a wealth of knowledge about what might motivate their child.

I'm particularly fond of social rewards that allow them to practice other skills. Many of my students have benefited from

- Earning "talk time" of 10 minutes with an adult or peer, where they can share whatever they wish to talk about. (This is where you will get to learn lots of trivia you can store away for the day you become a contestant on Jeopardy!)
- Computer time, alone or with a friend. Set parameters around what they can do on devices before offering this!
- Board game time with a friend
- Drawing time with a special drawing book and supplies (if possible)
- Extra reading time
- Being class photographer for the day
- Presenting to the class (for extroverts only)
- A Get-Out-Of card that enables them to skip a task with your agreement
- A reward for the whole class, like a favorite game, movie afternoon, or technology-based lesson. To reduce the potential for embarrassment with increased peer scrutiny, only you and the student should know this secret plan. If I were climbing a mountain, I'd hate someone taking a photo at my sweatiest moment!

Your Expectations

Students not only need to know what they are working toward earning, they also need to know exactly what you want them to do to earn it. Telling them what you want to see sets them up for success. Don't require too many things of them in order to earn the reward—we're asking them to scale just one mountain, not the entirety of the Himalayas. Pick one to three target goals. Make sure they are specific and achievable. Examples might include one to three of the following:

> **To see an example of an effective reward system in practice, watch Anxiety in School by Real Look Autism (Babble, 2012): https://youtu.be/utOLQkanm4Q**

- Using an indoor voice
- Raising their hand and waiting to be called
- Working for __ minutes before asking for help
- Asking for or taking a break when needed
- Getting out materials needed for a lesson
- Filing loose sheets
- Writing their agenda
- Packing their bag
- Bringing materials back to school
- Joining a peer in conversation or play at one recess a day

The Earning Schedule

Students also need to know how often they are expected to do what is being asked in order to get the reward. This is where we can be very flexible as educators.

Systems look different for different children. First, consider the appropriate duration for assessment. Don't ask a child who never does homework to complete homework for all five days of the week before they can have 10 minutes on a device. They won't do it. The view from the top isn't worth the effort to climb. Instead, some students may benefit from only being monitored for a behavior in one subject a day (Barkley, 2016). As they are successful, you can increase this to two subjects or more.

Some students might need more frequent reinforcement, like a prize or technology time for a short period every morning and afternoon. Barkley (2016) points out that immediately rewarding a skill is more effective at reinforcing what you want to see. Generally, you begin with more frequent reinforcement (e.g., daily) and then fade that over time or increase your expectations for what they must do to earn a reward on that timeline. Some teachers use a token economy, where students can earn tokens (e.g., stickers or checkmarks) toward a larger reward. In these cases, we also don't expect them to do 100% of what is asked to earn a reward. Maybe students have a daily checklist of three skills, and once they've demonstrated nine or more of these, they can redeem their tokens for 30 minutes of technology at the end of a day on a Friday. Whatever system you use, you want to match the size of the demand to the size/frequency of the reward.

Always, always give a reward once it is earned. We want the child to trust that if they keep up their end of the bargain, adults will too. Sometimes, parents or teachers might be faced with a dilemma: the child met the requirements for the reward system, but then either don't do another task we want them to do or they do something we don't like that is unrelated to the system. Do you give a reward? Yes, but you might want to delay temporarily to problem-solve a challenging behavior. Let them know why it's being delayed and when they will get it. Think of it this way: you've hired someone to cut your grass. They complete the task and come to you for payment, and you withhold it because they didn't also trim the hedges. That wasn't part of the deal! Will they want to cut your lawn in the future? No way!

When children lose out on rewards, it also reduces their motivation and makes it less likely they'll engage in the system going forward (Barkley, 2016). You might want to rig the system so they earn very easily at the beginning so they see what it feels like to be successful and earn the reward, and then gradually increase expectations. The side benefit of this is that, when you reward, rather than taking away, you are simultaneously building rapport.

Using a Reward System to Support Child Success

- Create (or have them create) visuals of their goals. This reduces the need to verbally remind them and gives you something to point to. It's very hard to argue with a routine that has been agreed upon and established! These visuals are even more effective if you can incorporate special interests. These can be whole-class, like our class bulletin board where Mario moved through what looked like a side-scroller video game landscape closer to a group reward each day, or individual. Sonia and I have created goal charts and checklists using students' favorite video game or cartoon characters to reinforce what they are working on at home or school. We've had students design their own visuals, using their illustration talents and making the representation of what they need to do more meaningful.

Children can draw what they need to do on schedules or goal charts to increase effectiveness.

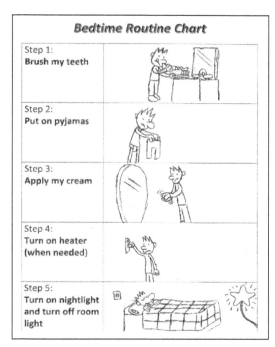

- Ongoing feedback can help them to know how close they are to the reward and what else they might need to do to get there. Use accountability language: "I'm looking forward to seeing you participate in math by answering one question!"

Sample Student Reward Charts

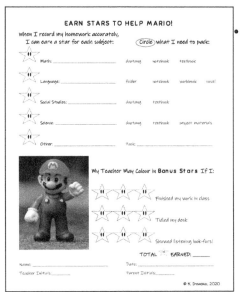

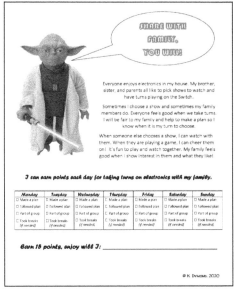

To increase demands, give students multiple opportunities in a row to be successful. Then during a check-in, say, "Well, we know you've mastered that skill! Wow! Let's add on to it. Now, let's see if you can also…"
- Not all children need a full reward system. Spontaneous rewards can also be effective. Give spontaneous rewards when you appreciate something they've done and want to increase the likelihood of seeing it again.
- Special interest breaks can be built into their schedule or issued occasionally as a spontaneous reward (e.g., "Wow, I love how hard you are working! Do you want to read for ten minutes?"). If they are routinely unfocused in a work

Effective Reward Systems

period, time how long they are actually on task; maybe it's five minutes. If they meet that, give them a short break to read a few pages of a book or work on a drawing. You can set a timer for them or let them know you'll check back in when the time is nearing the end. Gradually, increase how many minutes you expect them to work before earning a special interest break. You will probably find that, if you incorporate more breaks, they are more relaxed and willing to work in general!

Strategies for Building Student Self-Esteem and Relationships

---

Harness Interests to Build Self-Esteem

One of my students, Darryl, was often torn between attention-seeking in less-than-positive ways and really beautiful moments where he would help a struggling classmate with work or teach one of them how to play a board game. He had many talents, including knowledge of technology, cooking, music, and more. I began eliciting his help with tech set-up and problem-solving. I would show him pictures I took of food at restaurants. I'd include his song suggestions for song of the day. I'd write what he said on the board when it was a fabulous point.

Once he felt I really saw him, we were able to move ahead. I started giving him a goal of the day, usually related to having less wacky answers in class. He was certainly capable of making meaningful connections, but making classmates laugh was too highly motivating (though he couldn't always tell the difference between them laughing with him or laughing out of discomfort). We had a heart-to-heart, discussing the impact he wanted to have on classmates. We talked about how some of his choices didn't bring about what he wanted. Then I told him I wanted his peers to always see what I saw: someone who had a brilliant sense of humor, intelligence, and a kind heart. I gave specific examples of moments when he stood out: when helping peers, when helping me with technology, when his humor was appropriate, and when making meaningful connections during lessons. "Don't dull your shine!" I told him. He had a beautiful day and let Sonia and me know how hard he was trying. I sent a sunshine email home, I was so proud of him.

Interests Can Help Increase Awareness of Others

- Talk about your own goals and interests. Adults have them, too, and they're central to how all humans relate to others.
- Make time for ice-breaker conversation games in September and afterward, ideally on a weekly basis. This way students can mingle and discuss topics, getting to know peer preferences.
- Have students create posters of their strengths, talents, and positive qualities. Refer to these when you can and leave them posted, encouraging students to use peers as resources (Kluth & Schwarz, 2008). We want students with autism to notice that others also have expertise which they can access. No man is an island!
- Help students with autism identify peers with similar interests. Set up structured opportunities for them to partner and talk.

114   *Connecting through Strengths and Interests*

- Make a plan with the autistic student of one peer to approach to start a conversation. Brainstorm and write down questions they could ask them to get a conversation started. Be nearby to coach if needed.
- After you've listened patiently for a while, tell them how much you enjoy hearing about their interests, but you'd also like them to ask you (or a peer) about theirs, too. Explain that conversations are like a tennis match: reciprocal, with questions launching back and forth, giving the other person a chance to speak while remaining alert for when they will serve a question back!
- Encourage students in your class to play your autistic student's favorite games at recess at first. Once things are going well and they have a taste for being part of a game, increase your expectations. Teach the student with autism and peers how to negotiate which game to play at recess. This could be done by compromising (doing one game first and then the other), choosing different recesses, or combining games to create something unique.

Treat Them Like Experts

- Acknowledge their efforts and innovative thinking. Whole-class initiatives, like a class newspaper or independent study fair, are ways all students can present their knowledge while contributing to the group.
- Post their artwork.
- Invite them to present on a topic or teach a concept to the class.
- Gradually expand their interests. "Well, you know a lot about cheese-making. Can you find out what parts of the world cheese first appeared?" Sometimes this will occur naturally. Recently a student began asking his mom to show him how Pokémon worked because his new friend always talked about it. What a success!
- Consider what other skills related to their interest you can nurture. If they love video gaming, get them to write a review of their latest game.
- Tell them what you could see them doing in the future. "Maybe you'll run a computer support company!" "I could see you being a teacher one day."
- Get them to see themselves through a different lens. Ask them to picture their long-term success. Have them develop an action plan to achieve that goal. What skills will they need to develop? What do they already have? What can they work on now to help them? It is especially important that goals you mutually agree to work on in your class align with their priorities, rather than just yours. We want more than compliance: we want deep, meaningful growth.

Students draw their long-term goals.

Strategies for Building Student Self-Esteem and Relationships 115

Losing recess makes me feel embarrassed.

Please, don't yell!

Advice from Students

It is always my goal as a teacher to make my students understand how important their voices are. One of the highlights of the teacher workshops I run is when teachers hear testimonials from students. I wanted this book to reflect that, too, so I reached out to past and present students for their advice for teachers. Students range in age from 10 to 16. These are their own words, edited only for clarity or brevity.

What They Wish Teachers Wouldn't Do

- I dislike it when teachers single out a student or make an example of something they're doing—there's too much spotlight and sometimes it's just humiliating to go through.
- When they tell me to write stuff on the chalkboard because I feel embarrassed and when they yell at me when I get one question wrong.
- The bad thing is that, no offence, some teachers might scream if they get angry. That makes me feel upset.
- Overreacting in situations where it really isn't needed. When they snap at you, it makes you less motivated to do your work and you end up doing a poorer job because you keep that negativity in your mind.
- When teachers are very strict: blasting orders, not allowing us to do things on our own, when they are not flexible, and they assume I am doing things when I'm not.
- Some teachers are pretty serious during lessons and get upset when students don't listen. The second thing is that they say not to go on their phones while the students are supposed to be working, and yet they end up on their phones as well.
- Some lessons are too long so sometimes I lose focus. It feels like I am not understanding or remembering the lesson.
- Some teachers aren't straightforward and can be confusing.
- I don't like it when teachers talk too fast, call on you randomly, and just give you the work without explaining it.
- When teachers ramble on, I lose what they are trying to say and forget what is being taught and/or what I originally asked (when asking a question).
- In elementary, I didn't like being treated differently by the teachers. Examples: the expected work from me. It came across like I could not complete the work. Also, publicly being outed in class and treated differently for being different i.e. "everyone who has an IEP please come to the back of the class" etc. Not an environment conducive to learning.
- Missing recess for detention
- I don't like when teachers punish the whole class for something one student did. Instead they should deal with that one student
- I don't like when teachers hand out test papers in order by grade. It gives me anxiety since you don't know what grade you got and where your test is. Most of the time, my heart was thumping because I didn't know what grade I got. All I know is, the sooner you get your test, the higher your grade is.
- Giving lots of homework!
- I don't like when teachers give out homework that's really hard because I'll just stare at it and feel like I can't do it, and I feel bad.
- Surprise tests

- A thing I dislike is when you go to turn in a test, let's just say… math. There is a question that says, "Mary has 2 apples, Amy gives her 4, how many apples does Mary have?" 6. But you didn't say 6 <u>apples</u>, you just said 6 and your teacher LOSES IT. Tests are stressful enough. Why do they have to make it worse?

What They Appreciate Teachers Doing

- I like when my teachers joke around with me!
- I like when they are nice and accommodating.
- What I like about teachers: when they have a flexible mind, they're nice and caring because they understand us, they encourage us to keep learning, they want the best for us, and they are smart and very creative.
- Personally, I like it when teachers stay calm even if a situation is tense—it feels like they won't get mad for no good reason when they act like that.
- When they asked me in a polite way to stop doing certain things rather than just yelling.
- I like when teachers teach new things.
- I like it when they give you work and actually give you enough time to do it in class.
- When they are teaching the concept slowly, and they know that everyone has the idea before they move on.
- One day they teach the basics and then don't assign homework, and then the next day they go over the harder stuff and assign homework.
- I like it when I get to see things happen, like science experiments as I get to watch it, then learn about the fundamentals and how they did it.
- I like the way my teacher explains the lessons clearly. I like that we do lessons on the SMART Board.
- I like it when teachers use technology because it is easier to use and very easy to access. I like it when they help their students with work and help them understand.
- I like when my teacher uses the projector. My teacher also encouraged me and classmates to talk to one another.
- If I could design my day at school, we would watch videos on fun stuff and math and build up points to have rewards.
- Getting rewards for certain things
- I like the way they set motivation for students while teaching.
- I like when teachers *don't* say, "Oh good job!" or congratulate you for something they wouldn't normally for other students your age. It sounds like they think you're in Kindergarten.
- Teachers in high school treat me more like everyone else, like I'm independent. Whereas in grade school I was treated more like a child even as I got older. I appreciate when they use visual aids to support lesson i.e. PowerPoint presentations and YouTube videos; are direct with communication when asking a question in class; use a direct teaching style/simple; and are short and concise in teaching.

- I like when teachers give you the option of working with a partner or working alone. I like this because 1) I don't get anxiety about who to choose and when the teachers pair up the people who don't have a partner, I always end up with the bad ones, and 2) I know that all of the good people to work with are going to be taken.
- When there is a field trip, I get excited!
- I like when teachers assign calming activities like art or reading. It's a way to calm your brain from a stressful thing in your mind. It's a time where it's ok to be distracted. You can let your mind flow naturally.
- I like teachers who teach with a positive attitude. They make sure to teach the students so they know everything, and they also give advice if you need help. Maybe, if they do this, students will become teachers too.

These lists reflect student perspectives about what they've experienced in classrooms, as they understand it. It's possible they've misinterpreted teachers or not reflected on their own behaviors. That's important for us, as teachers, to know, too! Sometimes we have to do a better job of explaining our classroom decisions. While all students will vary in their preferences and dislikes, if you get to know your students, you'll have a better sense of who needs more positive reinforcement, who prefers a thumbs-up, who you may need to give a question in advance before calling on, who enjoys recording answers on the board, whether they will ask for help if they need it, etc. The lists also reflect commonalities: students dread feeling embarrassed or confused. They want that positive rapport, clear teaching, engaging lessons, and things to look forward to! Lucky for them, I think all teachers want their classrooms to have those things, too.

Final Thoughts

This book is not only about making the lives of students with autism better, it's about making yours better, too. When I teach new teachers, they have a lot of anxiety about getting it right. They want to know how to handle every possible situation they may encounter in their future classrooms. Experienced teachers know this feeling well, too. Whenever we get a new student whose student record file is thicker than our fist and whose reputation precedes them, we worry we don't have the resources. We worry we aren't enough for them.

Let me ease your burden a little. I want you to repeat what I'm about to tell you out loud. If it helps—or if you're on public transit right now—memorize it and recite it in the shower!

It's Okay Not to Know Everything

The reality is, we're much better equipped after each successive year of teaching. We get to the other side of each difficult situation and can approach the next one more confidently. We grow as we go.

There Is No One Right Way

If there was, that "best practice" would work every time. We use what we know—our education, experiences, intuition, drive to learn, talents, relationships with students—and craft thoughtful, individualized approaches. If they don't work, we go back to the drawing board. There is no one-size-fits-all in teaching. There is only what's right for each student.

You Are Not Alone

We have all been there. Don't feel embarrassed if things aren't working. Ask someone for help. In my research, I found that teachers most highly valued learning they gained from conversations and mentorship of other teachers. These might be very experienced teachers, or those newer to the profession who can bring fresh, innovative ideas. You have so much to gain and nothing to lose in reaching out.

You Are Part of a Community

The community is not just our classroom. We lose an invaluable gift as teachers if we remain an island unto ourselves. Create bonds with colleagues, those beginning in the profession, substitute teachers, and others. Your smile and greeting can make someone's day brighter. You also have expertise and ideas that could help someone else. When we share what works, we become stronger together. We all benefit.

Everyone Wants to Be Heard

That student with the giant record? Help them to feel a part of things. They crave connection, even if all the signals they are giving suggest they don't. They don't know any other way—yet.

You've Got This

If you can take away only one thing from this book, it's to teach from the heart and make decisions from a place of love. You have what you need to do this already. I know you care because you picked up this book!

Students Also Plant Seeds

We often think of the goal of education as student growth. We envision teachers as the ones planting seeds of curiosity and knowledge. While that is true, a hidden perk of the job is that we are also learning. With or without autism, no two students are the same and they all have something to contribute. Because of my students, I am a different teacher today than I was when I started. When I began focusing more on connection, there was an immediate decrease in power struggles. I learned to relax my schedule and listen to what my learners needed (within reason!). And teaching became much more fulfilling. I know you've had those moments, too. It's impossible to teach and not remember certain students who forever changed how you did something in the classroom. When we deeply connect, it is a transformative experience for students and teachers alike. May we always be open to the lessons children have to teach us.

Acknowledgments

If I had any doubt about the importance of connection, I only needed to write a book! This would have been an impossible task without the support of my whole family, especially my parents, my boyfriend, and my friends. My gratitude also to my faithful readers, Andrea and Sonia, for their suggestions. I'm thankful for my school staff and the multidisciplinary Autism Team in my school board. My dear colleagues who teach the same autism program as I do inspire me with their unrelenting curiosity for new tools to benefit our students and a readiness to share for the benefit of the team. A special thanks to Anne Wiley, who first brought me into her autism classroom in 2008, an experience that made me realize this was what I wanted to do.

I am grateful to my publisher, Mary Macchiusi, for believing in this book and for her generous guidance through each stage of the process. Writing a book is like putting your heart onto paper. I was fortunate to have an editor, Kat

Mototsune, who strengthened the heartbeat of this work considerably and made space in her own heart for it.

Thanks to my students who added their voices and artwork to this book.

This book would not have been possible without three people. First, my brother Danny, who fuels my work and who has taught me more than I've ever taught him. Second, Sonia Tran, who I am lucky to teach with every day and whose insights have always elevated my thinking. Her unwavering support helped me to envision this book—and myself as an author! Lastly, Shelley Murphy has always seen my path ahead more clearly than I have. Since I have known her, she has gently guided me toward new accomplishments, including speaking engagements, my doctorate, and teaching at the graduate level. Over the years, she made many remarks about the book she saw inside of me. Shelley also connected me to Pembroke. I can't string the words together adequately enough to thank you; so I will have to pay it forward. I hope to one day connect someone to their path the way you have done for me.

Kara and Danny

Professional Resources

Recommended Resources

This is by no means an exhaustive list of resources, but rather, readings I have enjoyed and recommend as an entry-point into a much larger field of works.

For Teachers/Parents

Tony Attwood

Attwood is the leading expert on the traits, strengths, and areas of need of children with autism with average to above-average cognitive abilities. His really *is* the complete guide: *The Complete Guide to Asperger's Syndrome*

Michelle Garcia Winner and Colleagues

Garcia Winner collaborates with others to produce a prolific body of work, available through socialthinking.com, that includes curricula, worksheets, books, games, webinars, and e-learning modules on using Social Thinking™ with people of all ages with social cognition difficulties. These resources are a good place to start:

Superflex: A Superhero Social Thinking Curriculum (S. Madrigal, M. Garcia Winner, & K. Knopp)
Why Teach Social Thinking?: Questioning Our Assumptions about What It Means to Learn Social Skills (M. Garcia Winner)
You Are a Social Detective!: Explaining Social Thinking to Kids (M. Garcia Winner, P. Crooke, & K. Knopp)

Ross Greene

Greene changed the way I conceptualized and responded to challenging behaviors and gave me effective tools to help my students to build skills. His website possesses many free resources and videos for parents and teachers:

The Explosive Child: A New Approach for Understanding and Parenting Easily Frustrated, Chronically Inflexible Children
Lost and Found: Helping Behaviorally Challenging Students (and, While You're at It, All the Others)
Lost at School: Why Our Kids with Behavioral Challenges are Falling through the Cracks and How We Can Help Them
Raising Human Beings: Creating a Collaborative Partnership with Your Child
The Walking Tour for Educators/Schools: https://www.livesinthebalance.org/educators-schools
The Walking Tour for Parents/Families: https://www.livesinthebalance.org/parents-families

Paula Kluth

I've enjoyed Kluth speaking on her work with students with autism and how to incorporate their interests to keep them engaged, motivated, and included throughout the day. Her books include even more of her tips:

"Just Give Him the Whale!": 20 Ways to Use Fascinations, Areas of Expertise, and Strengths to Support Students with Autism (P. Kluth & P. Schwarz)

You're Going to Love This Kid: Teaching Students with Autism in the Inclusive Classroom

Brenda Smith Myles and Colleagues

Want to challenge yourself to identify the unexplained, assumed-to-be-known social expectations across contexts? This book will help you change your lens:

The Hidden Curriculum for Understanding Unstated Rules in Social Situations for Adolescents and Young Adults (B. Smith Myles, M. Trautman, & R. Schelvan)

Teacher Resources on Emotional Regulation

Attwood, Tony. *Exploring Feelings: Cognitive Behaviour Therapy to Manage Anger*

— *Exploring Feelings: Cognitive Behaviour Therapy to Manage Anxiety*

Brukner, Lauren. *How to be a Superhero Called Self-Control!: Super Powers to Help Younger Children to Regulate their Emotions and Senses*

— *The Kid's Guide to Staying Awesome and in Control: Simple Stuff to Help Children Regulate their Emotions and Senses*

— *Self-Control to the Rescue!: Super Powers to Help Kids Through the Tough Stuff in Everyday Life*

Buron, Kari Dunn. *When My Worries Get Too Big: A Relaxation Book for Children Who Live with Anxiety*

Collins-Donnelly, Kate. *Starving the Anger Gremlin: A Cognitive Behavioural Therapy Workbook on Anger Management for Young People*

— *Starving the Anxiety Gremlin: A Cognitive Behavioural Therapy Workbook on Anxiety Management for Young People*

— *Starving the Stress Gremlin: A Cognitive Behavioural Therapy Workbook on Stress Management for Young People*

Huebner, Dawn. *What to Do When You Worry Too Much: A Kid's Guide to Overcoming Anxiety*

— *What to Do When You Grumble Too Much: A Kid's Guide to Overcoming Negativity*

— *What to Do When Your Temper Flares: A Kid's Guide to Overcoming Problems with Anger*

Kuypers, L. *The Zones of Regulation: A Curriculum Designed to Foster Self-Regulation and Emotional Control*

Murphy, Shelley. *Fostering Mindfulness: Building Skills That Students Need to Manage Their Attention, Emotions, and Behavior in Classrooms and Beyond*

First-Hand Accounts of Autism

Finch, David. *The Journal of Best Practices: A Memoir of Marriage, Asperger Syndrome, and One Man's Quest to Be a Better Husband*

Grandin, Temple. *Thinking in Pictures*

Higashida, Naoki. *The Reason I Jump: The Inner Voice of a Thirteen-Year-Old Boy with Autism*

McCreary, Michael. *Funny, You Don't Look Autistic: A Comedian's Guide to Life on the Spectrum*

Robison, John Elder. *Look Me in the Eye: My Life with Asperger's*

Read-Alouds for Children

I use a variety of books in my classroom to teach students of different age groups about autism, social-emotional themes like resilience, and general inclusion. With each group, I am mindful to select books most suited to the specific needs of the students. It is important to never disclose a diagnosis of a student without careful consideration and parent/student permission, and to carefully read books in advance to decide when and how to use them.

Understanding Diagnosis

Adams, Sue. *A Book about What Autism Can be Like*

Best, Cindy & Joyce Shor Johnson. *Meet Me Where I'm At*

Durà-Vilà, Glòria & Tamar Levi. *My Autism Book: A Child's Guide to Their Autism Spectrum Diagnosis*

Elder, Jennifer. *Different Like Me: My Book of Autism Heroes*

Espin, Roz. *Amazingly… Alphie!: Understanding & Accepting Different Ways of Being*

Etlinger, Rebecca. *To Be Me*

Gagnon, Elisa & Brenda Smith Myles. *This Is Asperger Syndrome*

Guglielmo, Amy & Jacqueline Tourville. *How to Build a Hug: Temple Grandin & Her Amazing Squeeze Machine*

Kluth, Paula & Patrick Schwarz. *Pedro's Whale*

Mosca, Julia Finley. *The Girl Who Thought in Pictures: The Story of Dr. Temple Grandin*

van Niekerk, Clarabelle. *Understanding Sam & Asperger Syndrome*

Rudolph, Shaina. *All My Stripes*

Sabin, Ellen. *The Autism Acceptance Book: Being a Friend to Someone with Autism*

Schnurr, Rosina G. *Asperger's, Huh? A Child's Perspective*

Steiner, Hartley. *It's Just a …What? Little Sensory Problems with BIG Reactions!*

Welton, Jude. *Can I Tell You about Asperger Syndrome?: A Guide for Friends & Family*

Picture Books for General Inclusion

Fleischman, Paul. *Weslandia*
Forler, Nan. *Bird Child*
Johnson, Chelsea, LaToya Council & Carolyn Choi,
    Intersection Allies: We Make Room for All
Ludwig, Trudy. *The Invisible Boy*
Myers, Christopher. *Wings*
Polacco, Patricia. *Thank You, Mr. Falker*
Woodson, Jacqueline. *Each Kindness*
— *The Day You Begin*
Zietlow Miller, Pat. *Be Kind*

Read-Alouds about Teasing, Bullying, and Peer Pressure

Binkow, Howard. *Howard B. Wigglebottom Learns about Bullies*
Clements, Andrew. *Jake Drake, Bully Buster*
Cook, Julia. *Bully B.E.A.N.S*
— *Peer Pressure Gauge*
— *Tease Monster*
Gervay, Susanne. *I Am Jack*
Ludwig, Trudy. *Confessions of a Former Bully*
— *The Invisible Boy*
— *My Secret Bully*
O'Neill, Alexis. *The Recess Queen*
Romain, Trevor. *Bullies are a Pain in the Brain*
Wilcox Richards, Nancy. *How to Handle a Bully*
— *How to Outplay a Bully*
— *How to Tame a Bully*

Read-Alouds for Social-Emotional Learning

Binkow, Howard. *Howard B. Wigglebottom Learns about Courage*
— *Howard B. Wigglebottom Listens to His Heart*
Black, Michael Ian. *I'm Bored*
— *I'm Sad*
— *I'm Worried*
Bland, Nick. *King Pig*
Carlson, Nancy. *How to Lose All Your Friends*
Cherry, Matthew A. *Hair Love*
Child, Lauren. *I Will Never Not Ever Eat a Tomato*
Cook, Julia. *Making Friends is an ART*
Curtis, Jamie Lee. *Today I Feel Silly & Other Moods that Make My Day*
DiPucchio, Kelly. *The Sandwich Swap*
Elovitz Marshall, Linda. *Rainbow Weaver*
Emberley, Ed & Anne Miranda. *Glad Monster, Sad Monster: A Book about Feelings*
Fergus, Maureen & Qin Leng. *And What If I Won't?*
Higgins, Ryan T. *We Don't Eat Our Classmates*

Javernick, Ellen. *What If Everybody Did That?*
Jeffers, Oliver. *Here We Are: Notes for Living on Planet Earth*
John, Jory. *The Good Egg*
Llenas, Anna. *The Colour Monster: A Pop-Up Book of Feelings*
Menchin, Scott. *Taking a Bath with the Dog and Other Things that Make Me Happy*
Newman, Lesléa. *Sparkle Boy*
Percival, Tom. *Ruby's Worry*
Saltzberg, Barney. *Beautiful Oops*
Scotton, Rob. *Splish, Splash, Splat!*
Spires, Ashley. *The Most Magnificent Thing*
Viorst, Judith. *Alexander and the Terrible, Horrible, No Good Very Bad Day*
Winn Lee, Britney. *The Boy with Big, Big Feelings*
Witek, Jo. *In My Heart: A Book of Feelings*

Novels for Social-Emotional Learning

Applegate, Katherine. *The One and Only Ivan*
Gantos, Jack. *Joey Pigza Swallowed the Key*
Palacio, R.J. *Wonder*
Patterson, James. *I Funny: A Middle School Story*
Sachar, Louis. *There's a Boy in the Girl's Bathroom*

Read-Alouds for Self-Regulation

Binkow, Howard. *Howard B. Wigglebottom Learns It's Okay to Back Away*
Cook, Julia. *The Anti-Test Anxiety Society*
— *A Bad Case of Tattle-Tongue*
— *Baditude! What to Do When Your Life Stinks!*
— *Bubble Gum Brain*
— *But It's Just a Game*
— *But It's Not My Fault*
— *Decibella and Her Six Inch Voice*
— *Don't Be Afraid to Drop*
— *I Am a Booger... Treat Me With Respect!*
— *I Can't Believe You Said That!*
— *I Can't Find My Whatchamacallit!!*
— *I Just Don't Like the Sound of NO!*
— *I Just Want to Do It My Way*
— *It's Hard to Be a Verb*
— *My Mouth is a Volcano!*
— *Personal Space Camp*
— *Planning Isn't My Priority... and Making Priorities Isn't In My Plans!*
— *Soda Pop Head*
— *Sorry I Forgot to ASK!*
— *Study Skilled...NOT!!!*
— *Teamwork Isn't My Thing, and I Don't Like to Share*
— *Thanks for the Feedback (I Think)*
— *That Rule Doesn't Apply to Me!*

Recommended Resources   125

— *The PROcrastinator*
— *Well I Can Top That!*
— *Wilma Jean the Worry Machine*
— *Winners Don't Whine and Whiners Don't Win*
— *The Worst Day of My Life...EVER!*
Greive, Bradley Trevor. *The Blue Day Book for Kids: A Lesson in Cheering Yourself Up*

MacLean, Kerry Lee. *Moody Cow Meditates*
Tracy, Kristina & Louise L. Hay. *I Think, I Am!*
Verde, Susan. *I Am Peace*
Young, Karen. *Hey Awesome*
— *Hey Warrior*

References

American Psychiatric Association. (2013). *Diagnostic and statistical manual of mental disorders* (5th ed.). Washington, DC: American Psychiatric Association.

Ansel, A., Rosenzweig, J. P., Zisman, P. D., Melamed, M., & Gesundheit, B. (2017). Variation in gene expression in autism spectrum disorders: An extensive review of transcriptomic studies. *Frontiers in Neuroscience, 10*, 601. https://doi.org/10.3389/fnins.2016.00601

Antezana, L., Scarpa, A., Valdespino, A., Albright, J., & Richey, J. A. (2017). Rural trends in diagnosis and services for autism spectrum disorder. *Frontiers in Psychology, 8*, 590. https://doi.org/10.3389/fpsyg.2017.00590

Ashburner, J., Ziviani, J., & Rodger, S. (2010). Surviving in the mainstream: Capacity of children with autism spectrum disorders to perform academically and regulate their emotions and behavior at school. *Research in Autism Spectrum Disorders, 4*(1), 18–27. https://doi.org/10.1016/j.rasd.2009.07.002

Attwood, T. (2007). *The complete guide to Asperger's syndrome.* London, UK: Jessica Kingsley Publishers.

Autism and Developmental Disabilities Monitoring Network Surveillance Year 2010 Principal Investigators. (March 28, 2014). Prevalence of autism spectrum disorder among children aged 8 years -- autism and developmental disabilities monitoring network, 11 sites, United States, 2010. *Surveillance Summaries, 63*(SS02), 1–21. https://www.cdc.gov/mmwr/preview/mmwrhtml/ss6302a1.htm

Avni, I., Meiri, G., Bar-Sinai, A., Reboh, D., Manelis, L., Flusser, H., Michaelovski, A., Menashe, I., & Dinstein, I. (2019). Children with autism observe social interactions in an idiosyncratic manner. *Autism Research.* https://doi.org/10.1002/aur.2234

Babble. (2012, September 21). *Anxiety in School | Real Look Autism | Babble*[Video file]. YouTube. https://youtu.be/utOLQkanm4Q

Baio, J., Wiggins, L., Christensen, D. L., et. al. (2018, April 27). Prevalence of autism spectrum disorder among children aged 8 years — autism and developmental disabilities monitoring network, 11 sites, United States, 2014. *Surveillance Summaries. 67*(6), 1–23. https://dx.doi.org/10.15585/mmwr.ss6706a1

Baker, J. (2008). *No more meltdowns: Positive strategies for managing and preventing out-of-control behavior.* Arlington, TX: Future Horizons.

Baker-Ericzén, M. J., Fitch, M. A., Kinnear, M., Jenkins, M. M., Twamley, E. W., Smith, L., Montano, G., Feder, J., Crooke, P., Garcia Winner, M., & Leon, J. (2018). Development of the supported employment, comprehensive cognitive enhancement, and social skills program for adults on the autism spectrum: Results of initial study. *Autism, 22*(1), 6–19. https://doi.org/10.1177/1362361317724294

Baldwin, S., Costley, D., & Warren, A. (2014). Employment activities and experiences of adults with high-functioning autism and Asperger's disorder. *Journal of Autism & Developmental Disorders, 44*(10), 2440–2449. https://doi.org/10.1007/s10803-014-2112-z

Barkley, R. A. (2012). *Executive functions: What they are, how they work, and why they evolved.* New York, NY: Guilford Press.

Barkley, R. A. (2016). *Managing ADHD in school: The best evidence-based methods for teachers.* Eau Claire, WI: Pesi Publishing & Media.

Baron-Cohen, S. (1995). *Mindblindness: An essay on autism and theory of mind.* Cambridge, MA: MIT Press.

Baron-Cohen, S., Richler, J., Bisarya, D., Gurunathan, N., & Wheelwright, S. (2003). The systemizing quotient: An investigation of adults with Asperger syndrome or high-functioning autism and normal sex differences. *The Royal Society Publishing, 358*(1430), 361-374. *https://doi.org/10.1098/rstb.2002.1206*

Baron-Cohen, S. (2012, September 12). The erosion of empathy. TEDx Talks. https://www.youtube.com/watch?v=nXcU8x_xK18

Barton, E. E. (2013). Premack principle. In: Volkmar F.R. (Eds.), *Encyclopedia of Autism Spectrum Disorders.* New York, NY: Springer.

Bauminger, N. & Kasari, C. (2000). Loneliness and friendship in high-functioning children with autism. *Child Development, 71*, 447–456. https://doi.org/10.1111/1467-8624.00156

Berenguer, C., Miranda, A., Colomer, C., Baixauli, I., Roselló, B. (2018). Contribution of theory of mind, executive functioning, and pragmatics to socialization behaviors of children with high-functioning autism. *Journal of Autism and Developmental Disorders, 48*(2), 430-441. https://doi.org/10.1007/s10803-017-3349-0

Beversdorf, D., Smith, B., Crucian, G., Anderson, J., Keillor, J., Barrett, A. M., Hughes, J., Felopulos, G., Bauman, M., Nadeau, S., & Heilman, K. (2000). Increased discrimination of "false memories" in autism spectrum disorder. *Proceedings of the National Academy of Sciences of the United States of America, 97*(15), 8734-8737. https://doi.org/10.1073/pnas.97.15.8734

Blumberg, S. J., Bramlett, M. D., Kogan, M. D., Schieve, L. A., Jones, J. R., & Lu, M. C. (2013). Changes in prevalence of parent-reported autism spectrum disorder in school-aged U.S. children: 2007 to 2011-2012. *National Health Statistics Reports, 65*(65), 1–11. https://files.eric.ed.gov/fulltext/ED582001.pdf

Booth, R., & Happé, F. (2010). "Hunting with a knife and ... fork": Examining central coherence in autism, attention deficit/hyperactivity disorder, and typical development with a linguistic task. *Journal of Experimental Child Psychology, 107*(4), 377–393. https://doi.org/10.1016/j.jecp.2010.06.003

Brock, J., & Bzishvili, S. (2013). Deconstructing Frith and Snowling's homograph-reading task: Implications for autism spectrum disorders. *The Quarterly Journal of Experimental Psychology, 66*(9), 1764-1773. https://doi.org/10.1080/17470218.2013.766221

Burnette, C. P., Mundy, P. C., Meyer, J. A., Sutton, S. K., Vaughan, A. E., & Charak, D. (2005). Weak central coherence and its relations to theory of mind and anxiety in autism. *Journal of Autism & Developmental Disorders, 35*(1), 63-73. https://doi.org/10.1007/s10803-004-1035-5

Cai, R. Y., Richdale, A. L., Dissanayake, C., & Uljarević, M. (2018). Brief report: Inter-relationship between emotional regulation, intolerance of uncertainty, anxiety, and depression in youth with autism spectrum disorder. *Journal of Autism & Developmental Disorders, 48*(1), 316–325. https://doi.org/10.1007/s10803-017-3318-7

Cappadocia, M. C., Weiss, J. A., & Pepler, D. (2012). Bullying experiences among children and youth with autism spectrum disorders. *Journal of Autism & Developmental Disorders, 42*(2), 266–277. https://doi.org/10.1007/s10803-011-1241-x

Center on the Developing Child (2011). *Building the Brain's "Air Traffic Control" System: How Early Experiences Shape the Development of Executive Function: Working Paper No. 11.* Harvard University. www.developingchild.harvard.edu.

Channon, S., Charman, T., Heap, J., Crawford, S., & Rios, P. (2001). Real-life-type problem-solving in Asperger's syndrome. *Journal of Autism & Developmental Disorders, 31*(5), 461-469. https://doi.org/10.1023/A:1012212824307

Chen, W., Landau, S., Sham, P., & Fombonne, E. (2004). No evidence for links between autism, MMR and measles virus. *Psychological Medicine, 34*(3), 543-553. https://doi.org/10.1017/S0033291703001259

Christensen, D. L., Baio, J., Van Naarden Braun, K., Bilder, D., Charles, J., Constantino, J. N., Daniels, J., Durkin, M. S., Fitzgerald, R. T., Kurzius-Spencer, M., Lee, L-C., Pettygrove, S., Robinson, C., Schulz, E., Wells, C., Wingate, M. S., Zahorodny, W., & Yeargin-Allsopp, M. (2016, April 1). Prevalence and characteristics of autism spectrum disorder among children aged 8 years — autism and developmental disabilities monitoring network, 11 sites, United States, 2012. *Surveillance Summaries. 65*(3), 1–23. https://dx.doi.org/10.15585/mmwr.ss6503a1

Clark, M. L. E., Vinen, Z., Barbaro, J., & Dissanayake, C. (2018). School age outcomes of children diagnosed early and later with autism spectrum disorder. *Journal of Autism & Developmental Disorders, 48*(1), 92–102. https://doi.org/10.1007/s10803-017-3279-x

Cook, A., Ogden, J., & Winstone, N. (2018). Friendship motivations, challenges and the role of masking for girls with autism in contrasting school settings. *European Journal of Special Needs Education, 33*(3), 302-315. https://doi.org/10.1080/08856257.2017.1312797

Courchesne, E., Carper, R., & Akshoomoff, N. (2003). Evidence of brain overgrowth in the first year of life in autism. *Journal of the American Medical Association, 290*, 337-344. https://doi.org/10.1001/jama.290.3.337

Crick, N. R., & Dodge, K. A. (1996). Social information-processing mechanisms in reactive and proactive aggression. *Child Development, 67*, 993–1002. https://doi.org/https://doi.org/10.2307/1131875

Croen, L. A., Zerbo, O., Qian, Y., Massolo, M. L., Rich, S., Sidney, S., & Kripke, C. (2015). The health status of adults on the autism spectrum. *Autism, 19*(7), 814–823. https://doi.org/10.1177/1362361315577517

Davidson, D., Vanegas, S.B. & Hilvert, E. (2017). Proneness to self-conscious emotions in adults with and without autism traits. *Journal of Autism & Developmental Disorders, 47*(11), 3392–3404. https://doi.org/10.1007/s10803-017-3260-8

De Martino, B., Harrison, N. A., Knafo, S., Bird, G., & Dolan, R. J. (2008). Explaining enhanced logical consistency during decision making in autism. *The Journal of Neuroscience, 28*(42), 10746–10750. https://doi.org/10.1523/JNEUROSCI.2895-08.2008

Dijkhuis, R. R., Ziermans, T. B., Van Rijn, S., Staal, W. G., & Swaab, H. (2017). Self-regulation andd quality of life in high-functioning young adults with autism. *Autism, 21*(7), 896–906. https://doi.org/10.1177/1362361316655525

Dymond, K. (2019). *Teacher insights: Self-efficacy and professional development needs related to supporting children with high-functioning autism* (Publication No. 13423645) [Doctoral dissertation, University of Toronto]. ProQuest Dissertations Publishing.

Elder, L. M., Dawson, G., Toth, K., Fein, D., & Munson, J. (2008). Head circumference as an early predictor of autism symptoms in younger siblings of children with autism spectrum disorder. *Journal of Autism & Developmental Disorders, 38*(6), 1104-1111. https://doi.org/10.1007/s10803-007-0495-9

Elder Robison, J. (2007). *Look me in the eye: My life with Asperger's.* New York, NY: Three Rivers Press.

Forrest, D. L., Kroeger, R.A., & Stroope, S. (2019). Autism spectrum disorder symptoms and bullying victimization among children with autism in the United States. *Journal of Autism & Developmental Disorders, 50*, 560–571. https://doi.org/10.1007/s10803-019-04282-9

Fox News (2016, April 4). 2 Arrested After Fight Over Crabs Legs Turns Violent, Police Say. *Fox News.* https://www.foxnews.com/

Frith, U. (1989). *Autism: Explaining the enigma.* Oxford, UK: Basil Blackwell.

Frith, U. & Snowling, M. (1983). Reading for meaning and reading for sound in autistic and dyslexic children. *British Journal of Developmental Psychology, 1*, 329-342. https://doi.org/10.1111/j.2044-835X.1983.tb00906.x

Gal, E., Landes, E., & Katz, N. (2015). Work performance skills in adults with and without high functioning autism spectrum disorders (HFASD). *Research in Autism Spectrum Disorders, 10*(Complete), 71–77. https://doi.org/10.1016/j.rasd.2014.10.011

Garcia Winner, M. (2007). *Thinking About You Thinking About Me* (2nd ed.). Santa Clara, CA: Think Social Publishing, Inc.

Garcia Winner, M. (2013). *Why teach social thinking?: Questioning our assumptions about what it means to learn social skills.* Santa Clara, CA: Think Social Publishing, Inc.

Garcia Winner, M. (14 Feb 2017). *How is teaching hidden rules different from teaching about expected/unexpected behavior?* Think Social Publishing, Inc. https://www.socialthinking.com/Articles?name=teach-hidden-rules-different-expected-unexpected

Gedek, H. M., Pantelis, P. C., & Kennedy, D. P. (2018). The influence of presentation modality on the social comprehension of naturalistic scenes in adults with autism spectrum disorder. *Autism, 22*(2), 205–215. https://doi.org/10.1177/1362361316671011

Grandin, T. (2006). *Thinking in pictures: And other reports from my life with autism.* New York, NY: Doubleday.

Green, S. A., Rudie, J. D., Colich, N. L., Wood, J. J., Shirinyan, D., Hernandez, L., Tottenham, N., Dapretto, M., & Bookheimer, S. Y. (2013). Overreactive brain responses to sensory stimuli in youth with autism spectrum disorders. *Journal of the American Academy of Child & Adolescent Psychiatry, 52*(11), 1158-1172. https://doi.org/10.1016/j.jaac.2013.08.004

Greene, R. W. (2008). *Lost at school: Why our kids with behavioral challenges are falling through the cracks and how we can help them.* New York, NY: Scribner.

Greene, R. W. (2014). *The explosive child: A new approach for understanding and parenting easily frustrated, chronically inflexible children.* New York, NY: Harper.

Hadjikhani, N., Åsberg Johnels, J., Zürcher, N. R., Lassalle, A., Guillon, Q., Hippolyte, L., Billstedt, E., Ward, N., Lemonnier, E., & Gillberg, C. (2017). Look me in the eyes: Constraining gaze in the eye-region provokes abnormally high subcortical activation in autism. *Scientific Reports, 7*, 3163. https://doi.org/10.1038/s41598-017-03378-5

Happé, F. G. E. (1997). Central coherence and theory of mind in autism: Reading homographs in context. *British Journal of Developmental Psychology, 15*, 1-12. https://doi.org/10.1111/j.2044-835X.1997.tb00721.x

Happé, F. & Frith, U. (2006). The weak coherence account: Detail-focused cognitive style in autism spectrum disorders. *Journal of Autism & Developmental Disorders, 36*, 5-25. https://doi.org/10.1007/s10803-005-0039-0

Hillier, A., Goldstein, J., Murphy, D., Trietsch, R., Keeves, J., Mendes, E., & Queenan, A. (2018). Supporting university students with autism spectrum disorder. *Autism, 22*(1), 20–28. https://doi.org/10.1177/1362361317699584

Howlin, P. (2003). Outcome in high-functioning adults with autism with and without early language delays: Implications for the differentiation between autism and Asperger syndrome. *Journal of Autism & Developmental Disorders, 33*(1), 3–13. https://doi.org/10.1023/A:1022270118899

Hviid, A., Hansen, J. V., Frisch, M., & Melbye, M. (2019). Measles, mumps, rubella vaccination and autism: A nationwide cohort study. *Ann Intern Med, 170*, 513–520. [Epub ahead of print 5 March 2019]. https://doi.org/10.7326/M18-2101

Hwang, S., Kim, Y. S., Koh, Y. J., Leventhal, B. L. (2018). Autism spectrum disorder and school bullying: Who is the victim? Who is the perpetrator? *Journal of Autism*

& *Developmental Disorders, 48*(1), 225–238. https://doi.org/10.1007/s10803-017-3285-z

Jacquemont, S., Coe, B. P., Hersch, M., Duyzend, M. H., Krumm, N., Bergmann, S., Beckmann, J. S., Rosenfeld, J. A., & Eichler, E. E. (2014). A higher mutational burden in females supports a "female protective model" in neurodevelopmental disorders. *American Journal of Human Genetics, 94*(3), 415–425. https://doi.org/10.1016/j.ajhg.2014.02.001

Jones, D. E., Greenberg, M., & Crowley, M. (2015). Early social-emotional functioning and public health: The relationship between kindergarten social competence and future wellness. *American Journal of Public Health, 105*(11), 2283–2290. https://dx.doi.org/10.2105%2FAJPH.2015.302630

Just, M. A., Cherkassky, V. L., Keller, T. A., & Minshew, N. J. (2004). Cortical activation and synchronization during sentence comprehension in high-functioning autism: Evidence of underconnectivity. *Brain, 127*(8), 1811-1821. Retrieved from https://doi.org/10.1093/brain/awh199

Kluth, P. (2018, October 26). Conference Presentation: "Just Give Him the Whale": Using Passions, Areas of Expertise & Strengths to Support Students on the Spectrum. Presented at the Geneva Centre for Autism Symposium, Toronto, ON.

Kluth, P. & Schwarz, P. (2008). *Just Give Him the Whale!": 20 Ways to Use Fascinations, Areas of Expertise, and Strengths to Support Students with Autism.* Baltimore, MD: Brookes Publishing.

Koolen, S., Vissers, C. T. W. M., Hendriks, A. W. C. J., Egger, J. I. M., & Verhoeven, L. (2012). The interplay between attentional strategies and language processing in high-functioning adults with autism spectrum disorder. *Journal of Autism & Developmental Disorders, 42*(5), 805-814. https://doi.org/10.1007/s10803-011-1310-1

Korpilahti, P., Jansson-Verkasalo, E., Mattila, M.-L., Kuusikko, S., Suominen, K., Rytky, S., et al. (2007). Processing of affective speech prosody is impaired in Asperger syndrome. *Journal of Autism & Developmental Disorders, 37*, 1539–1549. https://doi.org/10.1007/s10803006-0271-2

Lartseva, A., Dijkstra, T., & Buitelaar, J. K. (2015a). Emotional language processing in autism spectrum disorders: a systematic review. *Frontiers in Human Neuroscience, 8.* https://doi.org/10.3389/fnhum.2014.00991

Lee, M., Martin, G. E., Hogan, A., Hano, D., Gordon, P. C., & Losh, M. (2018). What's the story? A computational analysis of narrative competence in autism. *Autism, 22*(3), 335–344. https://doi.org/10.1177/1362361316677957

Le Sourn-Bissaoui, S., Caillies, S., Gierski, F., & Motte, J. (2011). Ambiguity detection in adolescents with Asperger syndrome: Is central coherence or theory of mind impaired? *Research in Autism Spectrum Disorders, 5*(1), 648-656. https://doi.org/10.1016/j.rasd.2010.07.012

Leekam, S. R., Nieto, C., Libby, S. J., Wing, L., & Gould, J. (2007). Describing the sensory abnormalities of children and adults with autism. *Journal of Autism & Developmental Disorders, 37*(5), 894-910. https://doi.org/10.1007/s10803-006-0218-7

Little, L. (2002). Middle-class mothers' perceptions of peer and sibling victimization among children with Asperger's syndrome and nonverbal learning disorders. *Issues in Comprehensive Pediatric Nursing, 25*,43–57. https://doi.org/10.1080/014608602753504847

Locke, J., Ishijima, E., Kasari, C., & London, N. (2010). Loneliness, friendship quality and the social networks of adolescents with high-functioning autism in an inclusive school setting. *Journal of Research in Special Educational Needs, 10*, 74–81. https://doi.org/10.1111/j.1471-3802.2010.01148.x.

López, B., Donnelly, N., Hadwin, J., & Leekam, S. (2004). Face processing in high-functioning adolescents with autism: Evidence for weak central coherence. *Visual Cognition, 11*(6), 673-688. https://doi.org/10.1080/13506280344000437

Lounds Taylor, J. (2017). When is a good outcome actually good? *Autism, 21*(8), 918–919. https://doi.org/10.1177/1362361317728821

Loveland, K. A., Pearson, D. A., Tunali-Kotoski, B., Ortegon, J., & Cullen Gibbs, M. (2001). Judgment of social appropriateness by children and adolescents with autism. *Journal of Autism & Developmental Disorders, 31*, 367–376. https://doi.org/10.1023/a:1010608518060

MacLennan, K., Roach, L., & Tavassoli, T. (2020). The relationship between sensory reactivity differences and anxiety subtypes in autistic children. *Autism Research, 000*, 1-11. https://doi.org/*10.1002/aur.2259*

Madrigal, S., Garcia Winner, M., & Knopp, K. (2008). *Superflex: A Superhero Social Thinking Curriculum.* Santa Clara, CA: Think Social Publishing, Inc.

Maïano, C., Normand, C. L., Salvas, M. C., Moullec, G., & Aimé, A. (2016). Prevalence of school bullying among youth with autism spectrum disorders: A systematic review and meta-analysis. *Autism Research, 9*(6), 601–615. https://doi.org/10.1002/aur.1568

Mamashli, F., Khan, S., Bharadwaj, H., Michmizos, K., Ganesan, S., Garel, K.-L.A., Ali Hashmi, J., Herbert, M.R., Hämäläinen, M. and Kenet, T. (2017). Auditory processing in noise is associated with complex patterns of disrupted functional connectivity in autism spectrum disorder. *Autism Research, 10*, 631-647. https://doi.org/10.1002/aur.1714

Matson, J. L. & Konst, M. J. (2013). What is the evidence for long term effects of early autism interventions? *Research in Autism Spectrum Disorders, 7*(3), 475–479. https://doi.org/10.1016/j.rasd.2012.11.005

Mayes, S. D., Calhoun, S. L., Aggarwal, R., Baker, C., Mathapati, S., Molitoris, S., & Mayes, R. D. (2013a). Unusual fears in children with autism. *Research in Autism Spectrum Disorders, 7*(1), 151-158. https://doi.org/10.1016/j.rasd.2012.08.002

Mayes, S. D., Gorman, A. A., Hillwig-Garcia, J., & Syed, E. (2013b). Suicide ideation and attempts in children with autism. *Research in Autism Spectrum Disorders, 7*(1), 109–119. https://doi.org/10.1016/j.rasd.2012.07.009

Mayes, S. D., Calhoun, S. L., Mayes, R. D., & Molitoris, S. (2012). Autism and ADHD: Overlapping and discriminating symptoms. *Research in Autism Spectrum Disorders, 6*(1), 277-285. https://doi.org/10.1016/j.rasd.2011.05.009

Mayes, S. D., Calhoun, S. L., Murray, M. J., Ahuja, M., & Smith, L. A. (2011). Anxiety, depression, and irritability in children with autism relative to other neuropsychiatric disorders and typical development. *Research in Autism Spectrum Disorders, 5*(1), 474-485. https://doi.org/10.1016/j.rasd.2010.06.012

McCrimmon, A. W., Altomare, A. A., Matchullis, R. L., & Jitlina, K. (2012). School-based practices for Asperger syndrome: A Canadian perspective. *Canadian Journal of School Psychology, 27*(4), 319–336. https://doi.org/10.1177/0829573512454991

Moye, D. (2016, February 9). Man Accused of Tossing Gator into Wendy's Drive-Thru Window. *The Huffington Post.* https://www.huffingtonpost.ca/

Mukaddes, N. M., & Fateh, R. (2010). High rates of psychiatric co-morbidity in individuals with Asperger's disorder. *The World Journal of Biological Psychiatry, 11*(2-2), 486–492. https://doi.org/10.3109/15622970902789130

Murphy, S. (2011). What I would do now: Supporting diverse readers in reading and writing. In D. Booth (Ed.), *Caught in the Middle: Reading and Writing in the Middle Years* (pp. 94–97). Markham, ON: Pembroke.

Murphy, S. (2014). (2014). Finding the Right Fit. *Young Children, 69*(3), 66–71. www.jstor.org/stable/ycyoungchildren.69.3.66

National Scientific Council on the Developing Child (2007). *The Timing and Quality of Early Experiences Combine to Shape Brain Architecture: Working Paper No. 5.* Harvard University. www.developingchild.harvard.edu.

Ormond, S., Brownlow, C., Garnett, M. S., Rynkiewicz, A., & Attwood, T. (2018). Profiling autism symptomatology: An exploration of the Q-ASC parental report scale in capturing sex differences in autism. *Journal of Autism*

& Developmental Disorders, 48(2), 389-403. https://doi.org/10.1007/s10803-017-3324-9

O'Riordan, M. A., Plaisted, K. C., Driver, J., & Baron-Cohen, S. (2001). Superior visual search in autism. *Journal of Experimental Psychology: Human Perception & Performance, 27*(3), 719-730. https://doi.org/10.1037/0096-1523.27.3.719

Pellicano, E. (2010). Individual differences in executive function and central coherence predict developmental changes in theory of mind in autism. *Developmental Psychology, 46,* 530-544. https://doi.org/10.1037/a0018287

Pellicano, E. (2012). The development of executive function in autism. *Autism Research & Treatment, 2012,* 146132. https://doi.org/10.1155/2012/146132

Plaisted, K. C. (2001). Reduced Generalization in Autism: An Alternative to Weak Central Coherence. In J. A. Burack, & T. Charman (Eds.), *The Development of Autism: Perspectives from Theory and Research* (pp. 139-169). Mahwah, NJ: Lawrence Erlbaum Associates.

Public Health Agency of Canada. (March 2018). *Autism spectrum disorder among children and youth in Canada 2018: A report of the national autism spectrum disorder surveillance system.* https://www.canada.ca/content/dam/phac-aspc/documents/services/publications/diseases-conditions/autism-spectrum-disorder-children-youth-canada-2018/autism-spectrum-disorder-children-youth-canada-2018.pdf

Pugliese, C. E., Anthony, L. G., Strang, J. F., Dudley, K., Wallace, G. L., Naiman, D. Q., & Kenworthy, L. (2016). Longitudinal Examination of Adaptive Behavior in Autism Spectrum Disorders: Influence of Executive Function. *Journal of Autism & Developmental Disorders, 46*(2), 467-477. https://doi.org/10.1007/s10803-015-2584-5

Remington, A. & Fairnie, J. (2017). A sound advantage: Increased auditory capacity in autism. *Cognition, 166,* 459-465. https://doi.org/10.1016/j.cognition.2017.04.002

Rosenthal, M., Wallace, G. L., Lawson, R., Wills, M. C., Dixon, E., Yerys, B. E., & Kenworthy, L. (2013). Impairments in real-world executive function increase from childhood to adolescence in autism spectrum disorders. *Neuropsychology, 27*(1), 13-18. https://doi.org/10.1037/a0031299

Safran, J. S., & Safran, S. P. (2001). The consultant's corner: School-based consultation for Asperger syndrome. *Journal of Educational & Psychological Consultation, 12*(4), 385–395. https://doi.org/10.1207/S1532768XJEPC1204_05

Safran, S.P. (2008). Why youngsters with autistic spectrum disorders remain underrepresented in special education. *Remedial & Special Education, 29*(2), 90–95. https://doi.org/10.1177/0741932507311637

Shattuck, P. T. (2006). The contribution of diagnostic substitution to the growing administrative prevalence of autism in US special education. *Pediatrics, 117*(4), 1028–1037. https://doi.org/10.1542/peds.2005-1516

Shattuck, P. T., Carter Narendorf, S., Cooper, B., Sterzing, P. R., Wagner, M., & Lounds Taylor, J. (2012). Postsecondary education and employment among youth with an autism spectrum disorder. *Pediatrics, 129*(6), 1042–1049. https://doi.org/10.1542/peds.2011-2864

Shepherd, C. A., & Waddell, C. (2015). A qualitative study of autism policy in Canada: Seeking consensus on children's services. *Journal of Autism & Developmental Disorders, 45*(11), 3550–3564. https://doi.org/10.1007/s10803-015-2502-x

Sinha, P., Kjelgaard, M. M., Gandhi, T. K., Tsourides, K., Cardinaux, A. L., Pantazis, D., Diamond, S. P., & Held, R. M. (2014). Autism as a disorder of prediction. *Proceedings of the National Academy of Sciences of the United States of America, 111*(42), 15220–15225. https://doi.org/doi:10.1073/pnas.1416797111

Smith, R. G., & Samdup, D. (2018). Update in development: Section b – autism spectrum disorder. In S. Piteau (Ed.), *Update in pediatrics* (pp. 207–221). Springer International Publishing. https://doi.org/10.1007/978-3-319-58027-2_7

Smith Myles, B., & Simpson, R. L. (2001). Understanding the hidden curriculum: An essential social skill for children and youth with Asperger syndrome. *Intervention in School & Clinic, 36*(5), 279–286. https://doi.org/10.1177/105345120103600504

Smith Myles, B., Trautman, M.L., & Schelvan, R. L. (2004). *The hidden curriculum for understanding unstated rules in social situations for adolescents and young adults.* Shawnee, KS: AAPC Publishing.

Southby, K., & Robinson, O. (2018). Information, advocacy and signposting as a low-level support for adults with high-functioning autism spectrum disorder: An example from the UK. *Journal of Autism & Developmental Disorders, 48*(2), 511–519. https://doi.org/10.1007/s10803-017-3331-x

Spratt, E. G., Nicholas, J. S., Brady, K. T., Carpenter, L. A., Hatcher, C. R., Meekins, K. A., Furlanetto, R. W., & Charles, J. M. (2012). Enhanced cortisol response to stress in children in autism. *Journal of Autism & Developmental Disorders, 42*(1), 75-81. https://doi.org/10.1007/s10803-011-1214-0

Sterzing, P. R., Shattuck, P. T., Narendorf, S. C., Wagner, M., & Cooper, B. P. (2012). Bullying involvement and autism spectrum disorders: Prevalence and correlates of bullying involvement among adolescents with an autism spectrum disorder. *Archives of Pediatrics & Adolescent Medicine, 166*, 1058–1064. https://doi.org/10.1001/archpediatrics.2012.790

Stichter, J., Herzog, M., Visovsky, K., Schmidt, C., Randolph, J., Schultz, T., & Gage, N. (2010). Social competence intervention for youth with Asperger syndrome and high-functioning autism: An initial investigation. *Journal of Autism & Developmental Disorders, 40*, 1067–1079. https://doi.org/10.1007/s10803-010-0959-1

Taylor, L. E., Swerdfeger, A. L., & Eslick, G. D. (2014). Vaccines are not associated with autism: An evidence-based meta-analysis of case-control and cohort studies. *Vaccine, 32*(29), 3623-3629. https://doi.org/10.1016/j.vaccine.2014.04.085

Top, N. D. Jr., Stephenson, K. G., Doxey, C. R., Crowley, M. J., Kirwan, C. B., & South, M. (2016). Atypical amygdala response to fear conditioning in autism spectrum disorder. *Biological Psychiatry: Cognitive Neuroscience and Neuroimaging, 1*(4), 308-315, https://doi.org/10.1016/j.bpsc.2016.01.008

Turner, L. B., & Romanczyk, R. G. (2012). Assessment of fear in children with an autism spectrum disorder. *Research in Autism Spectrum Disorders, 6*(3), 1203-1210. https://doi.org/10.1016/j.rasd.2012.03.010

Tranter, D. & Kerr, D. (2016). Understanding self-regulation: Why stressed students struggle to learn. *What Works? Research into Practice, 63*, Ontario Ministry of Education. http://www.edu.gov.on.ca/eng/literacynumeracy/inspire/research/ww_struggle.pdf

Tsang, V. (2018). Eye-tracking study on facial emotion recognition tasks in individuals with high-functioning autism spectrum disorders. *Autism, 22*(2), 161–170. https://doi.org/10.1177/1362361316667830

Uljarević, M., Nuske, H., & Vivanti, G. (2016). Anxiety in autism spectrum disorder. In L. Mazzone & B. Vitiello (Eds.), *Psychiatric symptoms of comorbidities in autism spectrum disorder* (pp.21-38). New York, NY: Springer.

Vanegas, S. B., & Davidson, D. (2015). Investigating distinct and related contributions of weak central coherence, executive dysfunction, and systemizing theories to the cognitive profiles of children with autism spectrum disorders and typically developing children. *Research in Autism Spectrum Disorders, 11*(Complete), 77-92. https://doi.org/10.1016/j.rasd.2014.12.005

Van Roekel, E., Scholte, R. H., & Didden, R. (2010). Bullying among adolescents with autism spectrum disorders: Prevalence and perception. *Journal of Autism & Developmental Disorders, 40*(1), 63–73. https://doi.org/10.1007/s10803-009-0832-2

Vermeulen, P. (2012). *Autism as context blindness.* Shawnee, KS: AAPC Publishing.

Vermeulen, P. (2018, October 25). Keynote: Autism and the Predictive Mind. Keynote presented at the Geneva Centre for Autism Symposium, Toronto, ON.

Vohra, R., Madhavan, S., & Sambamoorthi, U. (2017). Comorbidity prevalence, healthcare utilization, and expenditures of Medicaid enrolled adults with autism spectrum disorders. *Autism, 21*(8), 995–1009. https://doi.org/10.1177/1362361316665222

Weiss, D. (2015, January/February). Decoding neanderthal genetics. *Archaeology Magazine.* https://www.archaeology.org/issues/161-1501/features/2787-israel-neanderthal-epigenome-decoded

Wilbarger, J. L., McIntosh, D. N., & Winkielman, P. (2009). Startle modulation in autism: Positive affective stimuli enhance startle response. *Neuropsychologia, 47*(5), 1323-1331. https://doi.org/10.1016/j.neuropsychologia.2009.01.025

Xu, G., Strathearn, L., Liu, B., & Bao, W. (2018). Prevalence of autism spectrum disorder among US children and adolescents, 2014-2016. *The Journal of the American Medical Association, 319*(1), 81–82. https://doi.org/10.1001/jama.2017.17812

Zablotsky, B., Bradshaw, C. P., Anderson, C. M., & Law, P. (2014). Risk factors for bullying among children with autism spectrum disorders. *Autism, 18*(4), 419–427. https://doi.org/10.1177/1362361313477920

Index

4-Square, 50

accountability language, 102–103, 113
adaptability, 46
admonishments, 37
agenda writing, 75
anxiety, 8, 9, 16, 17, 46, 50, 54, 56, 76, 82–83, 84, 85, 99, 101, 111
alexithymia, 85
approachability, 67–68
arts, 31–32
Asperger Syndrome, 10, 18, 20, 54, 65
assessments, 11, 75–77
attention, 100–102
attention-averse, 101
attention-seeking, 100–101
autism
    causes, 19–20
    cognitive traits, 62
    co-morbid conditions, 19
    core difficulties, 11, 16–18
    described, 19–21
    development, 19
    diagnosis, 20–21, 38
    gender, 20, 37
    genetics, 19–20
    needs, 21
    neurodiversity, 21
    statistics, 20

autism lens
    described, 7–8
    hypothetical day, 11–16
    informed, 8
    social awareness, 36–37
    social situations, 34
    strengthening, 40
    theory of mind, 27
    wording test questions, 76
awareness of time, 72

basketball, 33
behaviors
    consequences, 95–98
    crisis management, 93–94
    maximizing outcomes, 98–103
    reasons for, 94–95
    reframing, 91–92
    when to stop talking, 92
    words to say, 92
big picture, 62
board games, 31
building understanding, 104
bullying, 53–55

categorizing, 42–43
challenging moments, 17
check-ins, 98–100
classroom culture, 87–88

classroom environment
    classroom culture, 87–88
    physical layout, 86
    sensory accommodations, 86–87
cognitive empathy, 25
cognitive flexibility, 64
cognitive learning style, 43–45
communication
    breakdown, 16, 22, 27
    challenges, 18, 52
    clear and direct, 45–46
    colleagues, 104
    digital, 25
    nonverbal, 26, 28
    parents and guardians, 75, 103
    pragmatic, 66
    removal of privileges, 98
    social, 24, 25, 56
community circles, 88
compliments, 101
conferencing, 99
connecting the dots, 45–46
consequences
    angry tone / raised volume, 95
    effective, 95–98
    ineffective, 95
    informing families, 96
    loss of privileges, 97–98
    parental involvement, 96–97
    routines, 96
    serious response, 97
    shaming, 95
    social repair, 95–96
    surveillance, 96
    suspensions, 95
    teaching and, 97
    unpredictable punishments, 95
context blindness, 41
control, 37
co-regulation, 84
COVID-19, 18
crisis management, 93–94
curriculum, 11

deception, 28–29
distilling information, 69
drama, 32

emotional regulation
    modeling self-care, 90
    talking about emotions, 88–89

    teaching new strategies, 89–90
emotions, 25–26, 88–89
empathy / empathizing, 25, 37
employment, 56
engagement, 109–110
equity versus equality, 87
executive dysfunction, 63–65, 67
executive functions, 63–64, 65, 66–67
eye contact, 26–27

family partnerships, 103–104
feedback, 87, 101–102, 113
feelings
    anxiety, 82–83, 84, 85
    dealing with, 82–85
    internalizing, 85
    phobias, 83
    words and, 84–85
fidgets, 86
figurative language, 68
flexibility, 46
fostering rapport
    benefits, 49
    described, 49–50
    strategies, 50–51

generalizing skills and situations
    categorizing, 42–43
    context blindness, 41
    difficulties, 41
    neurotypical learning, 40–41
goal chart, 100
goal-setting, 98–100
group work, 57–58

health, 32–33
hidden curriculum, 38–40, 73
hidden expectations, 38
hidden rules, 17, 38–40
History Organizer, 78
History Study Guide, 79
homework, 75
homographs, 66
honesty, 29
hypersensitivity, 81, 82
hyposensitivity, 81–82

ideas organization, 73–74
idioms, 28
imaginative strengths, 70
incentives, 110

inclusiveness, 59
independence, 18
inferencing, 68–69
inflexibility, 38
information processing
    executive dysfunction, 63–65
    weak central coherence, 63, 65
inhibition, 64
intentional instruction, 74–75
interdependence, 56
interests, 114–115
invisible disability, 23–25
invisible load, 10

joint attention, 26
journaling questions, 23–24
justice priorities, 29

language, 31–32
language organizers, 69, 71
language processing, 65–67
learning, 44
listening look-fors, 27
literal thinking
    adherence to rules, 29
    benefits, 29–30
    deception, 28–29
    honesty, 29
    interpreting information, 27–28
    justice priorities, 29
    logic, 29
literature circles, 32
logic, / logical thinking, 29, 37, 44–45
long-term outcomes, 56
long-term teaching, 47–48
losing, 33

Marshmallow Test, 63–64
materials management, 72–73
mathematics, 32–33
maximizing outcomes
    accountability language, 102–103
    check-ins and goal-setting, 98–100
    giving attention, 100–102
mind jars, 90
mindfulness activities, 31
motor skills and coordination, 17
music, 32, 86

neurotypical brains, 7, 27, 37
neurotypical learning, 40–41

note-taking, 70

open-ended tasks, 69–70
opinion-seeking, 30
organization, 17

parental / family involvement, 96, 103–104
peer buddies, 59
peer relationships, 60–61
personal space, 33
perspective-taking
    activity, 31
    challenges, 25–30
    language, social studies, and the arts, 31–32
    literal thinking, 27–30
    physical education, 33–34
    science, health, and math, 32–33
    short, engaging activities, 31
    social situations, 34
    strategies to build, 30–34
phobias, 83
physical education, 33–34
planning and organization
    managing materials, 72–73
    organizing ideas, 73–74
    time awareness, 72
play and socializing, 52–53
pragmatics / pragmatic language, 66
predictability, 67–68, 80–81
preparation, 46
privilege removal, 97–98
problem solving, 22–23, 89, 94
Problem-Solving template, 105

rapport, 49–51, 102
reading, 66–67, 70
recess, 7, 58
replacement thoughts, 90
response exemplars, 31
responsibility, 88
reward systems
    earning schedule, 111–112
    effective, 110–114
    expectations, 111
    feedback, 113
    incentives, 110
    possible rewards, 111
    reinforcement, 112
    social rewards, 111
    special interest breaks, 113–114
    spontaneous rewards, 113

supporting success, 112–114

visualizing goals, 112

rigidity, 29

routines, 38, 96

rules / rule-bound thinking, 37–38

school demands, 10–18

school landscape, 10

science, 32–33

selective mutism, 52

self-care, 90

self-esteem

as experts, 115

harnessing interests, 114

interests and awareness, 114–115

strategies for building, 114–118

student advice, 116–118

self-regulation, 84

sensory accommodations, 86–87

sensory processing

differences, 80–82

difficulties, 17

hypersensitivity, 81, 82

hyposensitivity, 81–82

predictability, 80–81

shaming, 95

short, engaging activities, 31

social confusion, 41

social differences

bullying, 53–55

described, 52–53

long-term outcomes, 56

play, 52–53

social and self-regulatory skills, 52

social gap, 56–57

social gap, 56–57

social issues, 16–17

social repair, 95–96

social rewards, 111

social situations, 34

social studies, 31–32

Social Thinking Methodology, 39

structure

assessments, 75–77

group work, 58

homework, 75

intentional instruction, 74–75

work periods, 75

student advice, 116–118

student experts, 115

student interest, 109–110

Student Reward Charts, 113

studying from notes, 71

sub-tasks, 72

suicide, 56

sunshine emails, 51

surveillance, 96

suspensions, 95

swearing, 39

systematizing, 37

talent, 108–109

teacher–student connection, 6–7

teaching strategies

approachability and predictability, 67–68

identifying what's important, 68–71

planning and organization, 72–74

structuring for success, 74–77

technology, 109

terminology, 18

theory of mind, 25, 27, 54

Tickets Out the Door, 35

time awareness, 72

transitions / transitioning, 72

Two Truths and a Lie, 23

unstructured times

group work, 57–58

inclusive climate, 59

recess, 58

verbalizing, 70

weak central coherence, 63, 65

Weekly Check-In, 107

When I'm Upset I Can…, 106

work periods, 75

working memory, 64

writing, 66–67

Zones of Regulation, 53